SAINT ATHANASIUS

*"Jesus said to them: Amen, Amen I say
to you, before Abraham was made, I am."*
—John 8:58

St. Athanasius portrayed as Bishop and
defender of the Catholic Faith.

SAINT ATHANASIUS

c. 297-373

THE FATHER OF ORTHODOXY

By

F. A. Forbes

"In the beginning was the Word, and the Word was with God, and the Word was God. The same was in the beginning with God. . . . And the Word was made flesh, and dwelt among us."
—John 1:14

TAN BOOKS AND PUBLISHERS, INC.
Rockford, Illinois 61105

Nihil Obstat: J.N. Strassmaier, S.J.
            Censor Deputatus

Imprimatur: Edmund Canon Surmont
            Vicar General
            Westminster
            August 5, 1919

Originally published in 1919 by R. & T. Washbourne, Ltd., London, as part of the series *Standard-bearers of the Faith: A Series of Lives of the Saints for Young and Old.*

ISBN 0-89555-623-5

Library of Congress Catalog Card No.: 98-61412

Cover illustration: St. Athanasius, by Brother Simeon, 1989. Copyright Monastery Icons 1989, Borrego Springs, California. Used by arrangement with Monastery Icons.

Printed and bound in the United States of America.

TAN BOOKS AND PUBLISHERS, INC.
P.O. Box 424
Rockford, Illinois 61105
1998

"Born of the Father before all ages, God of God, Light of Light, true God of true God, begotten not made, consubstantial with the Father . . . "

—From the Nicene Creed

St. Athanasius portrayed at his desk. From a miniature in a medieval manuscript in the Vatican Library.

CONTENTS

St. Athanasius, surrounded by members of his flock as he goes off into exile. Bishop of Alexandria and "The Father of Orthodoxy" against the Arian heresy, St. Athanasius was forced into exile five separate times by various Emperors for upholding the Catholic teaching that Christ is God.

SAINT ATHANASIUS

"I and the Father are one."

—Words of Our Lord
(*John* 10:30)

Chapter 1

A FORESHADOWING

THE Patriarch of Alexandria, Egypt was expecting company. He stood at the window of his palace looking down the long road, that at the first sign of his guests' arrival he might go forth and welcome them. Before him, like a white pearl in the blue waters of the Mediterranean, lay the city of Alexandria—"the beautiful," as men loved to call it. Across the harbor the marble tower of the great lighthouse soared up into the clear Eastern sky, white as the white cliffs of the Island of Pharos from which it sprang. It was noonday, and the sunshine lay like a veil of gold over all.

The Patriarch's thoughts were wandering in the past. He had been celebrating the anniversary of his holy predecessor Peter, the previous Bishop, who had won the crown of martyrdom during the terrible persecution of the Christians not so many years before. Several of the clergy present had come from afar to assist at the festival, and these were to be his expected guests.

The time of suffering was past and over, and yet it seemed to Alexander as if it had all happened yesterday and might happen again tomorrow. There stood the great palace of the Caesars, where the pagan emperor had sat in judgment upon the lambs of Christ's flock; there the famous temple of Serapis, where the Christians had been dragged to offer incense to the gods; there the amphitheater where they had been torn to pieces by beasts and slain with the sword for confessing the Name of Christ. And all through those dark days, firm and steadfast as the lighthouse on the cliffs of Pharos, had stood the Patriarch Peter, a tower of strength and comfort to his persecuted children.

A hundred Bishops and more had looked to him as their head, for the See of Alexandria in the East was second only to that of Rome in the West, and the burden of responsibility was heavy. But, thanks to the example of its chief, the Church in Egypt had borne the trial bravely, and if some had quailed before the torture and the rack and had fallen away, by far the greater number had been true. Even the unheroic souls, who had loved their lives better than their God, had not been lost beyond hope, for they had come back during the lulls in the storm, begging to be absolved from their sin. And Peter, mindful of his Master's words that he should not quench the smoking flax nor break the bruised reed, received them back, after they had done penance, into the fold of Christ with mercy and compassion.

There were some who had not scrupled to protest against such mercy. "Were these apostates," cried Meletius, Bishop of Lykopolis, "to be made equal to those who had borne the burden and the heat of the day?" And he had rebelled against the decision of the Patriarch and made a schism in the Church. Even the martyrdom of the holy Peter had not brought him back to his allegiance: the Meletians were rebels still, to the crying scandal of Christians and pagans alike.

They were a hard people to govern, these Alexandrians—subtle, passionate and unstable, ready to follow any preacher of novelties. Alexander half envied Peter his martyr's crown as he stood musing over the past.

What was delaying his guests? he wondered, as he looked down the long road, where there was as yet no sign of them.

On the shore, at a little distance, a group of boys were playing, their bare legs and white tunics flashing hither and thither as they ran. One of them, a tall slim lad, whose aureole of ruddy hair seemed to catch every wandering sunbeam, was evidently directing the game, for all seemed to look to him for orders. "A leader of men," smiled the Patriarch to himself, as a vigorous wave of the boy's hand brought all his companions round him.

They were building some kind of a platform now, on to which he of the ruddy locks was promptly hoisted, while the others appeared to be forming a procession.

"A church ceremony," murmured the Patriarch to himself, remembering his own boyhood days. Presently a little boy advanced solemnly and presented some kind of a vessel to the youthful bishop, who, with a magnificent gesture, beckoned to the procession to approach. Then, as the foremost boy advanced and knelt at his feet, he raised the vessel and poured some of its contents over his head.

"The baptism of the catechumens!" exclaimed the Patriarch; "but this looks a good deal too much like earnest!"

Hastily calling a servant, he bade him go down to the shore and bring up the band of boys who were playing there. Summoned thus hastily to appear before authority, they approached with some uneasiness, and there was a certain amount of scuffling among them which resulted in the appearance of the would-be bishop in the forefront of the group—and where should a bishop be if not at the head of his flock?

"What were you doing down there on the shore?" asked the Patriarch.

The boy's clear eyes looked at him with interest, but without a vestige of fear.

"We were playing," he said. "It was the baptism of the catechumens. I was the bishop, and they"—pointing to his companions—"were the catechumens."

"Are you a Christian?" asked Alexander.

"Yes," answered the boy proudly.

"And these?"

"Catechumens."

"What did you do?"

"I poured the water on them and said the words."

"What words?"

The boy repeated the formula in perfect Greek.

"Did you pour the water as you said the words?"

"Yes."

The Patriarch's face was troubled.

"It is a dangerous game to play at," he said. "What would you say if I told you that you had really baptized them?"

The boy looked at him in amazement.

"But I am not a bishop," he said.

The Patriarch could not help smiling.

"Although the bishop usually does baptize the catechumens," he said, "it is not necessary that it should be a bishop, not even necessary that it should be a priest."

The boy-bishop looked grave, his companions frightened, the Patriarch thoughtful.

"What is your name?" he asked suddenly, laying his hand on the ruddy locks.

"Athanasius," answered the boy.

"What would you like to be?" he asked.

"A priest," was the prompt answer.

"A bishop perhaps?" asked Alexander with a smile; "you think it is an easy and a glorious life?"

The boy's eyes looked straight into the Patriarch's.

"The blessed Peter was a martyr," he answered.

"You need much learning to be a priest."

"I love learning," said the boy.

Alexander noted the broad, intelligent brow, the keen eyes and the clear-cut face before him. His heart went out to this frank and fearless lad who loved the martyrs.

"Come to me this evening, and we will talk of this," he said, for his guests were at last to be seen approaching, and his duty lay with them.

That evening the boy and the Patriarch had much to say to each other as they walked under the palm trees in the garden of the episcopal palace. Alexander learned how Athanasius had been brought up in the Christian Faith under the shadow of the great persecution, among those who counted it the highest honor to shed their blood for Christ. He had been well taught in the famous Greek schools of Alexandria and was full of enthusiasm for the great Greek philosophers and poets. Strong of will, noble of heart and keen of intellect, the boy was born to something great—of that the Patriarch felt assured. The Church had need of such men in these troublous times, when the dangers of heresy had succeeded to those of persecution.

Alexander at once resolved to take Athanasius into his household and to bring him up as his own son, an inspiration for which he was often to thank God in the years to come. The boy soon grew to love the gentle and holy Patriarch, who could act with such strength and decision when it was needful for the good of the Church. He was constantly in touch with men of every rank and country, for Alexandria was a city where people of all nations and of all creeds met. Pagans, Jews and Christians lived side by side in their various quarters; there even existed a set of philosophers who tried to make a religion for themselves out of an amalgamation of several others.

Athanasius was still very young when he began to act as secretary to the Patriarch, accompanying him on all his journeys throughout his vast diocese; and he himself tells us how he stayed for a time among the monks in the desert of Egypt and how his young soul was set on fire by the holiness of their lives.

Neither science nor logic nor philosophy offered any difficulty to the brilliant young scholar, whose knowledge of Scripture and of theology was to astonish the men of his time. Alexander himself as he grew older leaned more and more on Athanasius, consulting him, young as he was, on the most important matters.

So the years rolled on, and the boy grew into manhood, "gentle and strong," as we are told by one who knew him, "high in prowess, humble in spirit, full of sympathy, angelic in mind and face." That he would make his mark on the world of his time, few who knew him doubted; but of the dauntless soldier-spirit that slumbered behind that gentle mien, of the steadfast will that no human power could shake, they knew but little. God's moment had not yet come.

Chapter 2

ARIUS THE HERESIARCH

THE night before the martyrdom of the Patriarch Peter, as he had lain in prison praying and waiting for that dawn which was to be his last on earth, there had come to him a few of his faithful clergy. They had braved many dangers to look once more upon the face of their beloved Bishop and to obtain his blessing and his last instructions; they had come also to plead for one who had asked their help.

But a short time before, a certain man called Arius had been excommunicated by the Patriarch for having joined the schism of Meletius. He it was who that very day had visited them, beseeching them with tears to use their influence with Peter to obtain his pardon. The clerics knew the tenderness of their Bishop's heart and his readiness to forgive the erring; they were therefore greatly surprised when their petition met with a stern refusal.

"Never," said Peter. "Arius is separated from the glory of the Son of God both in this world and in the next."

Then, as Achillas and Alexander, his dearest and most intimate friends, had drawn him apart to ask the reason for such unusual severity—

"This night," he said, "as I prayed, Our Lord appeared to me in glory, but His robe was rent from top to bottom. 'Who has treated Thee thus, my Lord!' I cried, 'and rent Thy garments?'

"'It is Arius,' He replied, 'who has torn My robe, and tomorrow they will come to you to intercede for him. Therefore I have warned you to keep him from the fold. But you shall die for Me tomorrow.'"

Then Achillas and Alexander, and they that were with them, prayed once more with their Bishop, and he blessed them and bade them depart in peace. And when the morning came, the promise of Christ was fulfilled, and His faithful servant received the martyr's crown.

Achillas succeeded Peter as Patriarch, and in course of time, yielding to the entreaties of Arius and deceived by his apparent good faith, he received him back into the fold and gave him charge of one of the largest churches in Alexandria in a district called Baukalis.

Tall and striking in appearance, with a certain eloquence and a great pretense of holiness, Arius soon became a popular preacher. He had even hoped, it was said, to succeed Achillas as

Patriarch; and when, on the death of Achillas, Alexander was elected to take his place, Arius' anger and envy knew no bounds. Since he could find no fault with the conduct of the new Patriarch, whom everyone acknowledged to be blameless and holy, he proceeded to find fault with his doctrine. "In teaching that Christ was the Eternal Son of God," said the priest of Baukalis, "Alexander and his clergy made a great mistake. Since Christ was the creation of God the Father, how could He Himself be God?"

It was a heresy that struck at the very roots of Christianity. Alexander remembered, too late, the warning of Peter. Gentle and peaceful by nature, he tried at first to win Arius by kindness. "Let him explain his difficulty," he said, "and discuss the question with theologians"; but all such suggestions were met with pride and obstinacy. Arius at last sent a haughty statement of his opinions, which were condemned by nearly all the Bishops of Egypt. He was therefore deposed and forbidden to preach, but he was not the man to take his defeat humbly.

Hastening to Caesarea in Palestine, where he had influential friends, he gave himself out as "the very famous, the much suffering for God's glory, who, taught of God, has acquired wisdom and knowledge." Many were seduced by his insidious persuasions, among them Eusebius, the

Bishop of Caesarea in Palestine, who, thoroughly taken in by the deceits and false holiness of the heretic, wrote a letter to Alexander in his favor.

The Patriarch replied by a detailed account of Arius' teaching and his trial, giving the reasons why the Synod had thought fit to depose him. This letter had an effect on the clergy and Bishops of Palestine which Arius was quick enough to see. He therefore retired into Syria, where he made great friends with another Eusebius, the clever and crafty Bishop of Nicomedia, who had gained an unfortunate influence over the Emperor.

It was now nearly twelve years since Constantine, himself a pagan, though the son of St. Helena, had prayed to the God of the Christians to give him the victory over his enemies. His prayers had been heard. In the brightness of the noonday sky there appeared a sign which outshone the sun in splendor—the image of the Cross of Christ. "In this sign thou shalt conquer" was traced in fiery letters across it, and the Emperor and all his army saw and believed.

With the Cross as standard, Constantine marched against his enemies and defeated them. From that day forth he became a catechumen and the protector and friend of the Christians. His first act was to publish an edict, the Edict of Milan, which gave them full liberty to practice their religion, build churches and preach.

Thus the Church came forth at last from the dark night of persecution, but her life on earth is ever a warfare against the powers of evil, and other dangers lay ahead.

The Emperor began by making humane laws. He abolished the punishment of crucifixion out of reverence for the Son of God, who had died upon the Cross, put a stop to the cruel games of the arena and bettered the condition of the slaves.

Constantine's nature was really a noble one, but there was much in him still of the pagan and the barbarian. Unfortunately for himself and for the world, he fell under the influence of Eusebius, Bishop of Nicomedia.

This man, who was said to have apostatized during the persecution of Maxentius and who had intruded himself, no one quite knew how, into the See of Nicomedia, had begun by winning the good graces of Constantia, the Emperor's sister. During the time when Constantia's husband, Licinius, was at war with her brother, Eusebius was his staunch friend, upholding him in his rebellion against the Emperor; but on the defeat of Licinius, the Bishop at once transferred his friendship to the conqueror, Constantine. Bishop Eusebius resembled Arius in his want of reverence and of honesty, and had taken Arius' side against the Patriarch, Alexander, praising openly the teaching of Arius and declaring that his only wish was that all men should share his opinions. He had even dared to write in Arius' favor to the Patriarch, declaring insolently that he had been unjustly deposed.

Alexander was growing old, but the Faith was in peril; it was a moment for vigorous action. Moreover, at his side, like a faithful watchdog, stood his secretary, the young deacon Athanasius. Circular letters were sent to Pope St. Sylvester and to all the Bishops warning them of the new danger that was threatening the Church. "Since Eusebius has placed himself at the head of these apostates," wrote Alexander, "it is necessary that it should be made known to all the faithful, lest they should be deceived by their hypocrisy."

Eusebius and Arius were both astonished and disgusted at the firm attitude of the Patriarch. Athanasius was at the bottom of it, they declared, and they vowed an undying hatred against him. The Emperor Constantine, who happened at this moment to be visiting Nicomedia, where he had spent a great part of his youth, heard Eusebius' version of the story. It was only a question of words, said the wily Bishop; what was really distressing about it was the spite and the venom with which the Patriarch of Alexandria had pursued an innocent and holy man for having dared to differ from him in opinion. Arius was then presented to the Emperor as a faithful and unjustly persecuted priest, a part which he knew how to play to perfection.

It was well known to Eusebius that the great desire of Constantine was to preserve and maintain peace in his empire. If this quarrel were allowed to go on, said the Bishop, there would soon be strife throughout the whole of the East, for there was much bitterness already. On the other hand, Constantine was known to all Christians as the protector and generous benefactor of the Church. Would it not be well for him, suggested Eusebius, to use his influence for good and to write to Alexander, bidding him lay aside this most unchristian dispute and make peace with Arius and his followers? The Emperor, as Eusebius had hoped, took alarm at the prospect of disunion in his dominions. A catechumen himself, and knowing but little of the great truths of Christianity, he was easily deceived by Eusebius' story and hastened to take his advice.

It was a scandalous thing, he wrote, that the peace of the Church should be disturbed for such a trivial matter. Let Alexander and Arius forgive one another; let them each keep their own opinion if they chose, but in concord and in quiet. He ended by begging both to give him peace by making peace among themselves and by putting an end to all such quarrels.

The letter was entrusted to Hosius, Bishop of Cordova, a confessor of the Faith, venerated throughout the Church for his wisdom and holiness. He was to deliver it personally to the Patriarch of Alexandria.

Now, Hosius was a Bishop of the Western Church and had heard but vague rumors of the doings of Arius and his followers in the East. His first interview with the Patriarch of Alexandria opened his eyes to the importance of the matter. It was no question of a war of words or a difference of opinion—Christianity itself was at stake; the Emperor must be warned, and warned at once. A letter was therefore written by the two Bishops, assisted probably by Athanasius, in which the Emperor was earnestly begged to take steps to summon a universal Council of the Church to decide the question. It was dispatched to him by a trusty messenger and in due time reached his hands.

Constantine, who was really anxious to do what was right, appealed to the Pope, St. Sylvester, to unite with him in summoning a Council. To the Bishops who were too poor to undertake a long journey with the usual attendance of clergy, the Emperor offered the necessary means. He undertook also to house and provide for the members of the Council as long as it lasted. The town of Nicea in Bithynia, about twenty miles from Nicomedia, was chosen as the meeting place. It was hoped by all devout Christians that peace and unity in the Church would be the result.

Chapter 3

THE GREAT COUNCIL

IN the early summer of the year 325 the
Council of Nicea met. Three hundred eigh-
teen Bishops were present, besides a multitude
of priests, deacons and acolytes. It was like the
Day of Pentecost, said the people: "men of all
nations and of all tongues."

Many bore the glorious marks of the sufferings they had endured for Christ; others were
wasted with long years of prison. There were the
hermit Bishops of Egypt, Paphnutius and Potamon, who had each lost an eye for the Faith;
Paul of Neo-Caesarea, whose muscles had been
burned with red-hot irons and whose paralyzed
hands bore witness to the fact; Cecilian of
Carthage, intrepid and faithful guardian of his
flock; James of Nisibis, who had lived for years
in the desert in caves and mountains; Spyrid-
ion, the shepherd Bishop of Cyprus, and the
great St. Nicholas of Myra, both famed for their
miracles.

Among the Bishops of the West were Theo-

philus the Goth, golden-haired and ruddy, who
had won thousands to the Faith; and Hosius the
Spaniard, known as "the holy," who had been
named by the Pope as his representative; together
with the two Papal Legates, Vito and Vincent.
Among those of the Eastern Church were the
venerable St. Macarius, Bishop of Jerusalem, and
St. Amphion, who had been put to the torture
in the reign of Diocletian.

Last but not least came the aged Patriarch of
Alexandria, the chief prelate of the Eastern
Church, who had brought with him as his assis-
tant the young deacon Athanasius.

Of the 318 Bishops present, seventeen, headed
by Eusebius of Nicomedia, were in sympathy
with Arius. They were but a small number, it is
true, yet Eusebius was the adviser of Constantine and the friend of his sister Constantia. He
relied on his influence with the Emperor and
his well-known powers of persuasion.

*   *   *   *   *

The day has come for the opening of the
Council. The Bishops and clergy are assembled
in a great hall which has been prepared for this
purpose. In the center, upon a splendid throne,
lies a copy of the Four Gospels, symbol of the
presence of Christ in the midst of His Church.
At the upper end a small gilt throne has been

erected for the Emperor, while the Bishops and the clergy sit on seats and benches running the whole way around the hall.

A quick whisper suddenly breaks the silence: "The Emperor!" and the whole assembly rises to its feet. Few of those present have seen the man whose name is on every lip, a Caesar and a Christian!

Alone and unattended, with bent head and humble mien, the Emperor crosses the threshold. A man of noble presence and of royal dignity, he wears the robe of Imperial purple blazing with gold and precious stones; the Imperial crown is on his head. There are some there who have seen that Imperial purple before, but under what different circumstances—"Hail, Caesar; those about to die salute thee!"

He advances slowly and with faltering footsteps between the ranks of Bishops standing to do him honor. Constantine the Great, the conqueror of the Roman world, trembles in the presence of these intrepid Confessors of the Faith who bear upon them the marks of the conflict. In the midst of that august assembly he, the catechumen, is as a little child. He will not even take his seat upon the throne prepared for him until the Bishops urge him to do so.

The Emperor speaks to them with deference and courtesy. It is not for him, he says, to dictate to them, for here he is but fellow servant with them of a glorious Lord and Master. They had met to preserve peace and concord in the Church and to put an end to all causes of strife. Let them do what they can to that end.

There are two men in that assembly on whom all eyes are bent. One of them is about sixty years of age, tall, thin and poorly clad, as one who leads an austere life. A wild shock of hair overshadows his face, which is of a deathly pallor; his eyes are usually downcast, owing to a weakness of sight. He has a curious way of writhing when he speaks, which his enemies compare to the wriggling of a snake. He is given to fits of frenzy and wild excitement, but has withal, when he chooses, a most winning and earnest manner, fascinating to men and women alike— Arius the heresiarch.

The other, seated on a low seat beside the Patriarch of Alexandria, is slight, fair and young; only his broad brow and keen, earnest eyes betray something of the spirit within; he shows no excitement. Serene and watchful, silent yet quick in his movements, he is like a young St. Michael leaning on his sword, ready to strike for the truth when the moment shall come—Athanasius the deacon.

The heresiarch is called upon to explain his doctrines. His discourse is long and eloquent.

He uses to the utmost his powers of fascination. He tries to hide the full meaning of his words under beautiful expressions, but his meaning is clear to all—"Jesus Christ is not God."

The Fathers and Confessors of the Faith, stricken with horror at the blasphemy, cry out and stop their ears. The indignation is universal. Eusebius and his party are in consternation. Arius has been too outspoken. He has stated his opinions too crudely; such frankness will not do here; he is no longer among the ignorant. Eusebius himself rises to speak and, with the insinuating and charming manner for which he is famous, tries to gloss over what Arius has said.

The Son of God is infinitely holy, he says, the holiest of all the creations of the Father and far above them all. Very, very close to the Father Himself, so close that He is very nearly God. As a matter of fact, he declares, the Arians believe all that the Church teaches.

A letter is produced and read by one of the prelates; it was written by Eusebius himself to a friend. Full of heresy, it shows most clearly the double-dealing of the Arian Bishop and his party. The indignation breaks out afresh, and the letter is torn to shreds in the presence of the Council. Even Eusebius is abashed, but there are others to take his place. The Arians continue the argument.

Silent and watchful at his post sits the young man who is destined to be the champion of the Faith through all the troublous years to come. He has not spoken yet, but now Alexander makes him a sign. The sword flashes from its scabbard; woe to those on whom its blows shall fall!

In a few words, sharp and clear as diamonds, Athanasius tears to pieces the veils in which the Arians had shrouded their true meaning. "Who has deceived you, O senseless," he asks, "to call the Creator a creature?"

He is the champion of Christ, the champion of the truth. The Bishops marvel at his words, which are as of one inspired; they thank God who has raised up so strong a bulwark against error. Alexander's eyes are aglow; it is for this that he has lived; he knew how it would be. His long life's work is nearly at an end; he can go now in peace. Athanasius is at his post.

But it is time to put an end to the discussion; Arius and his opinions are abhorred by everyone. A profession of Faith is drawn up by Hosius, the representative of Pope St. Sylvester, and presented for all to sign. It establishes forever the Godhead of Christ. To this day it is the profession of Faith of the whole Catholic world—the Nicene Creed.

"Born of the Father before all ages, God of God, Light of Light, true God of true God, begotten not made, consubstantial with the Father . . ."

The Emperor has listened earnestly to the discussion, following it as well as he can with his limited knowledge of doctrine. He approves the profession of Faith with his whole heart; let it be presented to all to sign.

But first—one moment—this heresy must be stamped out once and forever or there will be trouble in the days to come. An addition must be made before the signatures are affixed. It runs thus: "And if any say, 'There was a time when God was not; or if any hold that the Son is not of the same substance with the Father, or is . . . like a created being,' the Holy Catholic Apostolic Church condemns him, as it condemns forever Arius and his writings."

The text is then presented to the Bishops to sign. All are content but the seventeen Arians. The Emperor expresses his entire satisfaction with the decisions of the Council; he will uphold the law of the Church with the law of the State, he declares, and those who rebel will be punished.

The ranks of the Arians begin to waver; several Bishops sign the Creed; soon there are only five left—Eusebius at their head.

The Emperor speaks of banishment.

The argument is a powerful one. Eusebius wavers. He receives a message from Constantia bidding him give way; resistance is useless. He signs the profession in company with Theognis of Nicea, his friend.

Arius, with several of his supporters, is then condemned to banishment, and his writings are to be burned publicly. The minds of all are at rest. Several other matters of less importance are settled satisfactorily. The Council is at an end.

But Constantine has not finished with the Bishops. Today begins the twentieth year of his reign, a day kept with great rejoicing by the Roman Emperors. A banquet has been prepared at the palace; he claims the honor of entertaining the Confessors and Fathers of the Faith.

Times have changed indeed. The soldiers of the Imperial Guard salute with drawn swords the guests of the Emperor as they pass between them into the palace—that Imperial Guard who in other days, which many there remember, had dragged the Christians to torture and to death.

The Emperor receives them with veneration, kissing devoutly the scars of those who have suffered for the Faith. The banquet over, he begs their prayers and loads them with gifts, giving to each of the Bishops a letter to the governor of his province ordering a distribution of wheat to the churches for the use of the poor.

The hearts of all are full of joy and thankfulness. Taking leave of the Emperor, they return, each man to his own country. The Council of Nicea is over.

But there were two in whose hearts there was neither joy nor peace nor thankfulness; they were Eusebius of Nicomedia and Theognis of Nicea. Were they to return to their sees and confess themselves beaten? It would be a bitter home-coming. The officials of the palace were well known to Eusebius. He bribed the librarian to let him see once more the famous document that had just been signed by so many Bishops. Then, seizing a moment when the guardian's back was turned, the two Arians deleted their names from the profession of Faith and, return-ing home, continued to teach the doctrines which the Church had condemned. They counted on the protection of Constantia and her influence with the Emperor, but they were mistaken.

Three months after the Council of Nicea, Eusebius and Theognis were deposed by Alexan-der and the Bishops of Egypt, who elected Catholic prelates in their stead. The Emperor supported the decision of the Church, pro-nouncing a sentence of banishment on the rebels. "Eusebius has deceived me shamefully," he wrote to the faithful in Nicomedia.

Who could foresee that the Emperor, whose eyes were at last opened to the perfidy of his friend, would before long allow himself to be deceived more shamefully still by the very man whose dishonesty he had proved?

Chapter 4

THE CALM BEFORE THE STORM

WITH the enemies of the Church in exile, for a time there was peace. The heathen came flocking from every side to embrace the Faith. Pagan temples were overthrown and Christian churches were erected in their place. The Emperor himself built no less than eight in Rome, under the direction of Pope St. Sylvester, and furnished them with all that was required for the worship of God.

But Constantine was a stranger in the capital of his kingdom; he had spent his youth at the court of Nicomedia, and looked upon the East as his home. Rome, moreover, had tragic associations for him. It was there that he had caused his young son Crispus, falsely accused of treason by his stepmother Fausta, to be put to death. The young Caesar had been brave and upright and a favorite with all. Too late did his father learn that he was innocent. Fausta paid the penalty for her evil deed, but her death could not give life to the innocent victim.

Constantine resolved, therefore, to build himself an Imperial city in the land which he loved, far from the scene of the tragedy. He laid its foundations in Byzantium and gave it the name of Constantinople, or the city of Constantine. Everything was done to make the new capital the most magnificent city in the world. Works of art were brought from afar, the most skillful artists and builders were assembled from all the cities of Europe and of the East, enormous sums of money were spent, Christian churches were built; but Constantine could not give to his Imperial city what was wanting to himself—a pure and steadfast faith. Constantinople was destined to be the home of every heresy.

In the meantime the holy Patriarch Alexander had gone to his rest. As he lay on his deathbed he called for his beloved Athanasius, but there was no reply. Athanasius had fled from the city, fearing from certain words of the old man that he would be chosen to succeed him.

"Athanasius!" called the Patriarch once more.

There was one present who bore the same name, a not uncommon one in the East; they brought him to the bedside of the dying Bishop, but his eyes looked past him into space.

"Athanasius!" he called once more, "you think you can escape, but it shall not be so." And with these words he died.

The same thought had been in the hearts of all. Athanasius was known for his zeal and learning, his mortified life and his ardent love of God. He was young, it was true, but he was wiser than many older men. When the Bishops of the Church assembled to elect their new Patriarch, the whole Catholic population surrounded the church, holding up their hands to Heaven and crying, "Give us Athanasius!" The Bishops asked nothing better. Athanasius was thus elected, as St. Gregory tells us, by the suffrages of the whole people and by the choice of the Bishops of the Church.

It was a heavy burden to be laid on the shoulders of a young man scarcely thirty years of age. There were trials and combats ahead before which, if Athanasius had seen them, even his bold and undaunted spirit might have quailed. But the will of God, once made known to him, was accepted bravely. He would bear the burden with all the courage of his strong heart until the time came to lay it down.

The first few years of Athanasius' rule were years of peace during which he devoted himself to the work he loved, the conversion of the pagans and the visitation of his huge diocese, the Patriarchate of Alexander. He traveled from city to city confirming and strengthening the Church and making friends with the holy men over whom he had been called to rule.

One day, when he had been but a few months Patriarch, a message was brought to him from a stranger who wished to speak with him. His name was Frumentius, and he had traveled from a distant country. Athanasius was presiding at a meeting of Bishops. "Let him be brought in," he said, "and let him tell us what he desires."

The stranger was a man of noble bearing and gentle manners. He had a wondrous tale to tell. He and his brother Ædesius, left orphans at an early age, had been adopted by an uncle who was a learned man and a philosopher. Desiring greatly to undertake a voyage to Abyssinia to study the geography of the country and unwilling to interrupt the education of his two young charges, he took them with him, that they might continue their studies under his care. His work finished, he set sail for home with the two boys, but the boat, having put into a port for provisions, was set upon by savages, and everyone on board was killed.

Now, it happened that the boys had landed and were reading together under a tree on the shore. The savages had pity on their youth and, instead of killing them, carried them off and presented them to their King as slaves. The boys, who were intelligent and lovable, soon gained the affections of their barbarian master. Arrived

at manhood, they were given positions of trust
in the kingdom and loaded with every honor.
Frumentius, the elder, was especially beloved by
the King, over whom he gained a great influence for good. But the King fell sick and, being
near to death, called his wife, to whom he had
left the guardianship of his young son. "Let Frumentius help you in the government," he said;
"he is wiser and more faithful than any in the
kingdom."

The Queen Mother accordingly appointed Frumentius as the tutor of the young King, and
Governor of the State, while his brother Ædesius was given a less important position. Frumentius, whose earnest desire was to see the land
that he governed Christian, summoned all the
Christian merchants who came to trade in the
country and, giving them presents, begged them
to build houses of prayer and to do their utmost
to win the barbarians to the Faith. There were
many conversions, and by the time the young
King had reached his majority, several Christian
communities were scattered throughout the State.

His task being now at an end, Frumentius
asked leave to return to his own land with his
brother Ædesius. They had a hard task to persuade the King and the Queen Mother to let
them go, but at last they prevailed.

Frumentius, whose heart was yearning over

the country to which he owed so much, had come straight to the Patriarch of Alexandria to beg of him that he would send a Bishop to preside over the growing number of churches in Abyssinia and to preach the Faith in the districts where it was not yet known.

The Patriarch and the Bishops had followed the story with the greatest interest. When Frumentius ceased speaking, there was a moment of silence, broken suddenly by Athanasius himself.

"Who is more worthy of such a ministry," he cried, "than the man who stands before us?"

The suggestion was approved by all. Frumentius was ordained by the Patriarch, who gave him his blessing and bade him return to his mission. He was honored as a Saint in Abyssinia, where he labored zealously all his life for Christ. Ædesius, his brother, became a priest also and helped in the good work.

Athanasius, as we have already seen, had spent a part of his youth with the monks of the desert. It was his proudest boast that he had acted as acolyte to the great St. Antony. He resolved, therefore, to visit the district known as the Thebaid, where St. Pachomius, the father of monasticism in the East, had founded many monasteries and drawn up a rule for the monks.

Pachomius had been one of a body of young

soldiers seized against their will and forced to
fight in the wars between Constantine and Maxentius. It happened one day during a journey
that they landed at Thebes in Egypt, where they
were treated with harshness and cruelty. Hun-
gry, poorly clad and miserable, the young soldiers were lamenting their ill fortune when a
party of strangers approached them from the
town, welcoming them as friends and brothers
and giving them food, garments and all that they
so badly needed.

"Who are these good men?" asked Pachomius
of a bystander.

"They are Christians," was the answer. "They
are kind to everyone, but especially to strangers."

"What is a Christian?" persisted the young
soldier.

"A man who believes in Jesus Christ, the only
Son of God, and does good to all," was the
reply.

Pachomius reflected for a few minutes and
then withdrew a little way from his companions. "Almighty God, who have made Heaven
and earth," he cried, lifting his hands to Heaven,
"if You will hear my prayer and give me a knowledge of Your Holy Name, and deliver me from
the position in which I am, I promise You that
I will consecrate myself to Your service forever."

Not long after, Pachomius was set free and,

seeking out a Christian priest, received Baptism and instruction. Then, going at once to the cell of an old hermit called Palemon, famous for his holy and mortified life, he knocked at the door of his hut.

"Who are you, and what do you want?" asked the old man, opening his door a few inches.

"I am called Pachomius, and I want to be a monk," was the answer.

"You cannot be a monk here," said Palemon. "It is a hard thing to be a true monk, and there are few who persevere."

"Perhaps so," replied Pachomius; "but all people are not alike."

"I have already told you," repeated the old man, "that you cannot be a monk here. Go elsewhere and try; if you persevere you can come back."

"I would rather stay with you," said Pachomius.

"You do not know what you are asking," answered Palemon. "I live on bread and salt; I pray and do penance the greater part of the night—sometimes the whole night through."

Pachomius shivered, for he was a sound sleeper, but he replied sturdily enough:

"I hope in Jesus Christ that, helped by your prayers, I shall persevere."

Palemon could resist him no longer. He took the young man to live with him and found him a humble and faithful disciple. After some years, the two hermits went together to the desert of the Thebaid and began the work to which God had called Pachomius, for Palemon died soon after.

Many monasteries were founded, and men flocked to the desert to give themselves to God. They slept on the bare ground, fasted continually and cultivated the barren earth or made baskets and mats of the coarse reeds that grew in the marshes, selling them for the profit of the poor. Twice during the night the weird blast of the horn that summoned them to prayer broke the vast silence of the desert.

Hearing of the arrival of Athanasius, Pachomius came down from his lonely monastery of Tabenna, surrounded by his monks; but he hid himself among them from humility, or from the fear that Athanasius would do him too much honor. The Saint, however, detected the Saint, and they were soon firm friends. To the Patriarch, the monks of Egypt represented all that was best and strongest in the national spirit. On these men he knew he could rely, and his hopes were not disappointed. The solitaries of the desert, to a man, would be faithful to Athanasius during the years of trial that followed.

Indeed, wherever Athanasius went throughout his vast diocese, the hearts of all loyal and noble men went out to him instinctively. He was a precious gift of God to Egypt—a precious gift of God to the whole Catholic Church.

Pachomius and the hermit

Chapter 5

FALSE WITNESSES

THE storm of persecution which was to fall with such fury upon St. Athanasius was already gathering.

Constantia, the Emperor's favorite sister, who had always been strongly in favor of the Arians, became very ill. The priest who attended her on her deathbed, a friend and tool of Eusebius of Nicomedia, induced her to persuade Constantine, who visited her continually during her illness, that Arius and his friends had been unjustly condemned and that the judgment of God would fall on him and his empire in consequence. Constantine, always easily influenced by his immediate surroundings, began to waver. Constantia soon died, but the Arian priest continued the work that had been so successfully begun. Arius believed all that the Church believed, he pleaded; let him at least be allowed to come into the presence of the Emperor; let him have a chance to prove his innocence.

Although Constantine had heard with his own

ears the blasphemies of the heresiarch, although he had approved so heartily of the decision of the Council which condemned him and had enforced it with the power of the State, he gave way before the persuasions of this stranger.

"If Arius can assure me that he believes the profession of Faith set forth by the Council of Nicea," he said, "he may return."

The good news was instantly made known to the heretic and his friends, and Arius hastened to Constantinople, where he was admitted into the Emperor's presence.

"Is it true that you believe what the Church teaches?" asked Constantine.

"I take my solemn oath that I believe what I hold in my hand," replied Arius, unfolding the Nicene Creed.

In the hollow of his palm was concealed a statement of his own false doctrines, but this the Emperor could not know. He professed himself satisfied, and thus the seed was sown which was to bring forth bitter fruit during centuries to come.

With Arius recalled, there was no longer any reason why Eusebius and Theognis, who declared that they shared his opinions, should remain in banishment. Once in Constantinople, Eusebius regained all his old influence over the Emperor.

From that day forth, the Constantine of the

heavenly vision, the Constantine of the Council of Nicea, noble, wise and humble, disappears from the pages of history, and a man changeable, capricious and uncertain takes his place.

The first act of Eusebius and Theognis was to drive out the Catholic Bishops who had been elected to replace them in their sees; the second was to look about them to see who was likely to stand in their way. Eustathius, the Bishop of Antioch, an intrepid defender of the Faith, must be gotten rid of at once, they decided, and they proceeded to plot his ruin.

They started for Jerusalem to visit—or at least, so they said—the beautiful Church of the Holy Cross which the Emperor had just built. On their way home, they announced that they would stay for a short time at Antioch, and they invited all the Bishops who were likely to be friendly to meet them there in council. They were received with the greatest courtesy by Eustathius, who did all that he could to make their visit pleasant. They had, however, bribed an abandoned wretch of the town to enter while the council was sitting and accuse Eustathius before all present of a scandalous crime.

Affecting to be greatly grieved and horrified at the accusation, they deposed Eustathius and elected an Arian in his place, silencing those who opposed their unjust and unlawful conduct by declaring that they acted by command of the Emperor. Constantine was then appealed to, but in vain. The Arians were all-powerful.

The next obstacle to be removed was Athanasius, but Eusebius was clever enough to realize that this would be no easy task. Athanasius was not only the chief Bishop of the Eastern Church, but one who had defeated the Arians several times before on their own ground.

He began by writing a letter to the Patriarch in which he informed him that Constantine, having learned that the views of Arius were quite correct, had been pleased to recall him from banishment. It was only just and fair, therefore, that Athanasius should receive him into communion; Eusebius, indeed, had reason to know that the Emperor would be greatly displeased if he refused to do so.

Athanasius' reply to this threatening message was short and decided. Neither threats nor persecution, he said, would induce him to go against the decrees of the Council of Nicea. Arius had been condemned by the universal Catholic Church; by that decision all true Catholics must stand.

Eusebius was not at all discouraged. He wrote to the Emperor and told him how lightly the Patriarch had treated his wishes. "Athanasius is much too young for such a responsible position," he wrote, "and is of a quarrelsome and obstinate temper. He is the last man in the world to fill a post which, if peace is to be kept in the Church, requires the greatest tact and charity." Perhaps, he suggested, if the Emperor himself were to write to him, he might be made to see the matter in a different light. A threat of banishment is always a powerful argument.

On receiving this letter, the Emperor—to his shame, be it said—wrote to the Patriarch as follows: "Being informed of my pleasure, admit all who wish to communion with the Church. If I hear of your standing in the way of any who seek it, I will send at once those who will depose you from your see."

The reply of the Patriarch was firm and courageous. "It is impossible," he answered, "for the Catholic Church to hold communion with those who deny the Divinity of the Son of God and who are therefore fighting against Him."

Eusebius was absent when the letter arrived, and the changeable Constantine was favorably impressed by its noble and fearless tone; the matter was therefore dropped.

Eusebius, still determined on the Patriarch's ruin, looked about him for a tool. He found the Meletians—always troublesome and ready to join in a plot against those in authority. Three of them, appearing suddenly at Nicomedia where Constantine was then staying, accused Athanasius of having usurped the Royal power by levying an unlawful tax upon the people. Unfortunately for the success of this little plot, there were present at Court at that moment two priests of Alexandria who were able to prove to the Emperor that the Patriarch was completely innocent. Constantine even wrote a letter to Athanasius telling him of the false charge brought against him, severely blaming those who had made it and inviting him to come himself to Nicomedia.

This was not at all what Eusebius wanted. He could not prevent the arrival of Athanasius; he therefore set to work once more to prejudice Constantine against him before he came. The Meletians were pressed into service again, and accused the Patriarch of treason. He had sent a purse of gold, they said, to a certain rebel, who had stirred up a rising against the Emperor. But when Athanasius appeared at Nicomedia, he was able to prove that the story was a falsehood; and, to the disgust of Eusebius and his party, he returned to Alexandria bearing a letter from the Emperor fully establishing his innocence and the perfidy of his accusers.

Rumors of what was passing had even reached St. Antony in his desert solitude, and the old man, on hearing of all that his friend and dis-

ciple had had to suffer, came down from his
mountain cave to praise him for his courage and
to speak to the people.

"Have nothing to do with the Arians," he
said; "you are Christians, and they say that the
Son of God is a creature." Crowds came flocking to see the old man, for all had heard of his
miracles and of his holiness. He blessed them
all and exhorted them to hold fast to the true
faith of Christ, so steadfastly upheld by their
Patriarch, after which, having done the work he
had come to do, he returned to his solitude.

The Arians were still plotting. Some time
before, when Athanasius had been visiting that
part of his diocese called the Mareotis, he had
heard that a certain Ischyras, who gave himself
out as a priest although he had never been validly
ordained, was causing scandal. He celebrated, so
people said, or pretended to celebrate, the Holy
Mysteries in a little cottage in the village where
he lived, in the presence of his own relations
and a few ignorant peasants. Athanasius sent one
of his priests, called Macarius, to inquire into
the matter and to bring the impostor back with
him.

Macarius, on his arrival, found Ischyras ill in
bed and unable to undertake the journey. He
therefore warned one of his relations that the
sick man had been forbidden by the Patriarch

to continue his so-called ministry, and departed. Ischyras, on his recovery, joined himself to the Meletians, who, urged on by the Arians, were moving heaven and earth to find a fresh charge against Athanasius. On hearing his story, they compelled him by threats and by violence to swear that Macarius had burst in upon him while he was giving Holy Communion in the church, had overturned the altar, broken the chalice, trampled the sacred Host underfoot and burned the holy books. They reported that all this had been done by order of the Patriarch.

Once more Athanasius had to defend himself, and once more he triumphantly cleared himself of the accusation brought against him.

In the first place, as he proved to the Emperor, there was no church in the village where Ischyras lived. In the second, the man himself had been ill in bed. In the third, even if he had been up and well, he could not have consecrated, since he had never been validly ordained. Ischyras himself, not long after, escaping from the hands of the Meletians, swore in the presence of thirteen witnesses that he had been induced by threats to bear witness to the lie.

But the failure of this plot was only the signal for hatching another. A certain Meletian Bishop called Arsenius, whom Athanasius had deposed for refusing to obey the decrees of the

Council of Nicea, was induced to hide himself away in the desert. The Meletians then gave out that he had been murdered by order of the Patriarch, who kept his withered hand for purposes of magic. A wooden box was even produced containing a hand which was said to be that of the dead man.

Constantine seems to have believed the story, for he summoned Athanasius to come to Antioch to stand his trial, at which Eusebius and Theognis of Nicea were to preside. Athanasius did nothing of the sort. He sent trusty men into the desert to make a diligent search for the missing Arsenius, who, after some difficulty, was found. The fact was made known to the Emperor, who wrote once more to the persecuted Patriarch, affirming his innocence and threatening the Meletians with severe punishment if they invented any more calumnies against him. Arsenius himself, having repented of his part in the matter, asked pardon of Athanasius and promised obedience for the future.

Chapter 6

A ROYAL-HEARTED EXILE

ATHANASIUS had prevailed once more over his enemies, but Eusebius was always at the Emperor's side and knew how to play upon his weakness. Was it possible, he asked, that so many and such various charges could be brought up against a man if he were innocent? Athanasius was clever and had many friends, he continued, who were ready to swear that black was white for his sake. Let him be forced to appear alone before his accusers, and the Emperor would soon find out the truth. As a matter of fact, such charges could only be dealt with by a council; let one be held at once, and let Athanasius be summoned to attend.

Constantine fell into the trap. A council was summoned, and letters were sent to Alexandria. Athanasius, however, clearly saw that he could expect no justice in the midst of his enemies, and for a long time refused to leave his see. In the meantime the place of meeting had been changed from Caesarea to Tyre, and Athanasius

was accused by Eusebius of having obstinately
resisted the Emperor's orders. His reasons, they
added, were plain to all; conscious of his guilt,
he dared not face the assembly. The Emperor
threatened to send and bring him by force if he
did not come. Further resistance was useless, so
he set out for Tyre.

It was a strange Council. Of the sixty Bishops present, nearly all were Arians and open enemies of Athanasius. The Meletians were also
present. Jailers were at the doors instead of deacons. The priest Macarius, to whose innocence
Constantine himself had testified, was brought
in guarded by soldiers and loaded with chains.
Athanasius himself was obliged to stand as a
criminal before his judges. A few of the Egyptian Bishops who were present loudly protested
against such behavior, but their protests were
insultingly set aside.

The old charges were brought up one by one.
Athanasius was accused of being violent and cruel
in conduct, a perpetual center of strife. To this
he answered that the trial was not a fair one,
considering that nearly all who were present were
his enemies.

The affair of Ischyras was then brought up,
but nothing could be proved.

Lastly, a Meletian Bishop told, with thrilling
and tragic details, the story of the cruel murder

of Arsenius.

"Here is the very hand of the murdered man," he concluded, producing and opening the famous box. A cry of well-feigned horror burst from the Arians.

"Did any of you know Arsenius?" asked Athanasius calmly. Several rose to their feet. "Then, behold my witness," said the Patriarch, signing to a priest who stood near the door.

A man was brought in whose face and figure were hidden in a long cloak, which Athanasius drew slowly away. It was Arsenius himself who stood before them!

"Here is one hand," continued the Patriarch, drawing it out from the cloak, "and here is the other. I presume that to no man God has given more. Perhaps those who maintain that that severed hand is the hand of Arsenius can show us where it was affixed."

There was a moment of general confusion, during which the Meletian who had so graphically told the story of Arsenius' murder concluded that prudence was the better part of valor and hastily disappeared from the assembly. But the Arians were never at a loss. It was by magic, they declared, that Athanasius had caused the dead man to appear in their midst.

It was useless to continue the argument against such persistent injustice. Athanasius left the

Council abruptly and set out for Constantinople to place himself, a stern and accusing figure, in the Emperor's way as he rode out from his palace.

Constantine, recognizing who it was, tried to pass in silence, but Athanasius stood firm.

"The Lord judge between me and you," he said solemnly, "if you take the part of my enemies against me."

The Emperor halted. "What do you wish?" he asked.

"Let me be tried by a lawful council, or let me meet my accusers face to face in your presence," said Athanasius.

"It shall be done," replied Constantine.

The Arians, meanwhile, had declared Athanasius guilty of all the charges brought against him and had deposed him from his see. They were congratulating themselves on the success of their enterprise when they received an alarming letter from the Emperor accusing them of concealing the truth and bidding them come at once to Constantinople. Several of them, seized with fear, returned to their homes; a few others, who were bolder, headed by Eusebius and Theognis of Nicea, set out for the Imperial city. They made their plans on the way. Once arrived, instead of bringing up the old charges, they accused Athanasius of having prevented the sailing of the grain vessels from Alexandria to Constantinople in order to cause a famine. It was a clever trick. Constantine was extremely touchy about the prosperity of his new city and had just condemned to death a friend of his own for the same crime. He turned on Athanasius in anger.

"How could I, a poor man and a Bishop, do such a thing?" asked the Patriarch.

"You are rich enough and powerful enough for anything," retorted Eusebius bitterly.

As for Constantine, he declared that he would uphold the decisions of the Council. Athanasius deserved to lose his life, but he would show indulgence. He therefore banished him to Treves in Gaul, and the Arians triumphed.

There was mourning and lamentation in Alexandria and throughout all Egypt when the tidings came. Many appeals were made for justice, but in vain. Even St. Antony, though he wrote to Constantine, could not move him. One thing alone the Emperor would not do in spite of all the persuasions of the Arians—appoint a successor to the absent Patriarch. Athanasius, indeed, continued to govern the diocese from his distant exile, writing continually to his Bishops and clergy, exhorting them to stand fast in the Faith and reminding them that the road to consolation lay through affliction.

Eusebius, in the meantime, was trying to force Alexander, the aged Bishop of Constantinople, to admit Arius to communion. Although ninety years old, he stood firm, and neither threats nor persuasions could move him. The Emperor was at last induced to fix a day on which Alexander was to receive the heretic or be driven from his see.

The Bishop appealed to Heaven. He ordered a seven days' fast throughout his diocese, during which the faithful were to pray that God would prevent such a sacrilege. On the eve of the appointed day, the aged prelate, having heard that Arius had arrived in the town, prostrated himself on his face before the altar. "Lord," he prayed, "if Arius must be received to communion in this church tomorrow, take me, I beseech Thee, from this world. But if Thou hast pity on Thy Church, suffer not, I pray Thee, that such a thing should be."

Arius at that very moment was being escorted in triumph around the city by his followers. Suddenly the heresiarch turned pale and trembled. He did not feel well, he said; he would rejoin them presently. The time passed, and he did not return. At last they went to look for him. It was but a dead body which they found, a sight before which even they turned pale. Arius had been overtaken by a sudden and horrible death.

The fate of the heresiarch made a great impression on the Emperor, who had himself but a short time to live. During his last illness he was haunted by the thought of Athanasius. His eldest son, Constantine II, who held his court at Treves, was a firm friend of the exiled Bishop; the dying Emperor sent him a secret message to restore Athanasius to his see. He then received Baptism at the hands of Eusebius of Nicomedia, and died a few days later.

Constantine's empire was divided between his three sons, Constantine, Constans and Constantius. The two former, who were staunch friends of Athanasius, would die within twelve years of their father. Then Constantius, who had inherited all the weakness and none of the good qualities of Constantine the Great, and was, moreover, the tool of the Arians and the bitter enemy of those who were true to Athanasius, would be left master of the whole Roman Empire.

One of the first acts of Constantine II was to bring Athanasius back to Alexandria. He had been absent for over two years, and the rejoicings attending his return were great. They were not to last long, however, for Egypt and the East made up that part of the Empire which had been left to Constantius, who was completely in the toils of Eusebius.

Now, Eusebius had long been coveting the see

of Constantinople; he therefore proceeded, with the Emperor's assistance, to depose the rightful Bishop and to install himself in his place. He was, as he thought, in a position to carry all things before him, when Athanasius, firm and undaunted as ever, appearing suddenly on the scene, upset all his plans. Both Constantine and Constans were Athanasius' friends, and Constantius was not strong enough to resist them.

Eusebius determined to take a bold step—he would appeal to the Pope, and he promptly set to work to compose a letter which was a masterpiece of deceit.

"Athanasius has been deposed by a Council of the Church," he wrote. "His return was therefore unlawful." An account of all the charges brought against the Patriarch at the Council of Tyre followed. "Ink does not stain the soul," observed Eusebius lightly, as lie after lie took shape upon the paper.

The letter was sent to Rome by three trusty friends, but Pope Julius was not so easily deceived. He knew more about the matter than the Arians thought—so much, indeed, that the chief of the three envoys left suddenly during the night, fearful of what might come to light on the morrow. The two others, losing their heads completely, agreed to meet Athanasius at a synod at which the Pope himself should preside.

Eusebius was beside himself when he heard of this arrangement. To appear in some Western town, with no Emperor to back him up, and to urge against Athanasius, in the presence of the Pope, charges which he knew to be false, was a program which did not appeal to him at all. Taking the law into his own hands, he called a council of his friends and elected an Arian called Gregory in Athanasius' place.

Even if the Patriarch had been rightly deposed, the Egyptian Bishops alone could have elected his successor; but Eusebius and his party had long since ceased to care for right or justice. Theodore, the Governor of Egypt, was known to be a good Catholic and friendly to Athanasius. He was therefore removed, and an apostate called Philagrius, notorious for his violence and cruelty, was put in his place. The first act of this man was to publish an edict stating that Gregory was the Patriarch of Alexandria and that Athanasius was to be treated as an enemy. With armed troops he then took possession of the city churches, while Gregory, with a strong escort of soldiers, made his entrance into the town. All who resisted were imprisoned, scourged or slain.

To prevent further bloodshed, Athanasius left Alexandria and set out for Rome. The first news that he heard on reaching Italy was that his friend and patron Constantine II was dead.

Chapter 7

THE DAY OF REJOICING

IT was an evil day for Alexandria. Most of the Egyptian Bishops refused to acknowledge Gregory and were instantly arrested. Some were banished, some tortured, some imprisoned. St. Potamon, who had narrowly missed martyrdom during the persecution of Diocletian, was scourged with rods until he died. The many cruelties of the usurper made him so hateful to the Alexandrians that, after four years of tyranny, he was killed by the mob in a sudden outbreak of fury.

Athanasius, in the meantime, had made his way to Rome, where he was received by St. Julius I as a champion of the Faith. The case should be tried in his own presence, the Pope declared; but it was impossible to get the Arians to Rome. Excuse followed excuse, pretext followed pretext. Eusebius, the head of the Arian party, died at last in his usurped see, but his spirit survived in his followers. They drew up a creed of their own and sent it to the Pope, who rejected it at the Council of Milan. The Nicene Creed was the confession of Faith of the Catholic Church, he said. But the Nicene Creed, which proved so fully the divinity of Christ, was just what the Arians would not accept.

A fresh Council was called at Sardica, at which they were at last induced to be present. But when Athanasius was proved innocent, and the Bishops whom the Arians had banished appeared to bear witness to the violence and cruelty with which they had been treated, the Arians abruptly left the Council and returned to Philippopolis. Here they formed a council of their own, in which they not only excommunicated Athanasius, but had the impudence to "excommunicate" Pope Julius himself.

The Council of Sardica, at which were present the orthodox Bishops of Italy, Spain, Gaul, Africa, Greece, Palestine and Egypt, was very well able to get on without them. The innocence of Athanasius was finally established, the Arians and their creed condemned. A circular letter was then written to all the Churches, informing them of what had passed, and legates were dispatched to the two Emperors, Constans and Constantius.

Constantius dared not resist. Urged by his brother, who did his best to show the conduct of the Arians in its true light and threatened

him with civil war if he persisted in upholding
them, he sent letters to Alexandria ordering that
Athanasius should be honorably received. Gregory had met his death a short time before, so
there was no obstacle to Athanasius' return.

The Alexandrians, in the meantime, had
received a letter from Pope Julius in praise of
their Patriarch. "If precious metals," he wrote,
"such as gold and silver, are tried in the fire,
what can we say of so great a man, who has
been through so many perils and afflictions, and
who returns to you having been declared innocent by the judgment of the whole Synod?
Receive, therefore, beloved, with all joy and glory
to God, your Bishop Athanasius."

Never had Alexandria seen such rejoicings.
The people thronged forth from the city to meet
their exiled Patriarch, singing hymns of rejoicing, waving branches of trees and throwing rich
carpets upon the road along which he was to
pass. Every little hill was crowded with people
thirsting for a sight of that beloved face and figure. It was six years since they had seen him,
and what had they not suffered during his
absence?

As for Athanasius, his one thought, as usual,
was to establish his people in the Faith. Those
who had been led astray by the Arians were par-
doned and received with the greatest charity. The

weak ones who had given in through fear were strengthened with tender forbearance. Those who had been Athanasius' enemies were greeted as friends on their first sign of repentance. For the time, the Arians were defeated; they could do nothing. Constans was too strong for them.

The present moment was the Patriarch's, and he determined to use it to the full. The Bishops of Egypt gathered around him; widows and orphans were provided for, the poor housed and fed and the faithful warned against false doctrines. The churches were not large enough to hold the crowds that flocked to them. It was a time of peace which God vouchsafed to His people to strengthen them for the coming storm.

New Bishops were consecrated, men of holy life who could be trusted. Even the monks in their distant monasteries received inspiring letters from their Patriarch, stirring them up to realize the ideals of the spiritual life and to pray for the peace of the Church. For in the midst of all his labors Athanasius still found time to write—letters against the Arians, treatises in defense of the Faith and on the religious life, brilliant, strong and convincing. It was necessary to be vigilant, for the Arians were everywhere trying to seduce men by their false doctrines, teaching that Christ was not God. Letters from Athanasius were a powerful weapon in defense of the truth.

So the years passed in incessant prayer and labor, until the whole of Egypt was strong and steadfast in the Faith. "The Saints of the fourth century were giants," says a modern writer, "but he of Alexandria was the greatest of them all."

The time was coming in which his work was to be tried as gold in the fire. Constans was killed in battle, leaving Constantius master of the whole empire. It was a moment for misgivings; but for some time the new Emperor seemed favorably disposed, even going so far as to assure Athanasius of his friendship. It was a friendship which might well be mistrusted.

Pope Julius had also died and had been succeeded by Liberius. One of the first acts of Constantius was to write to the new Pope, offering him handsome presents and urging him to condemn Athanasius. Letters from the Arians containing all the old charges followed, but in vain. Liberius refused with indignation both presents and requests.

A fresh persecution broke out. Athanasius, it is true, was not molested, but his enemies were only waiting for a pretext to attack him. This pretext they soon found.

At Easter of the year 354, the churches of Alexandria were so crowded with worshippers that there was scarcely room to breathe. It was proposed to Athanasius that he should hold the Easter services in a large church that had been lately built but was not yet dedicated. Athanasius hesitated to do this without leave, as it was built on the Emperor's property, but he was at last persuaded by the people to yield. The Patriarch Alexander had done the very same thing, they urged, in the Church of St. Theonas on just such an occasion; in a case of necessity it was certainly lawful. But they had counted without the Arians, who instantly accused Athanasius of having usurped the royal authority.

The Patriarch, in his famous "Apology to Constantius," stated the reasons for his act, but it was useless; other false charges were scraped up against him, and his doom was sealed. In the spring of the next year, Constantius, who was now master of both the East and the West, succeeded by force of persecution in inducing the members of a large council, which he had had summoned at Arles in France, to condemn Athanasius as guilty. The Emperor himself was present with his troops and threatened with drawn sword those who resisted his will. The Bishops who refused to sign were scourged, tortured or exiled; the Pope was banished to Berea, where he was treated with harshness and cruelty.

In the winter of the next year, a General called

Syrianus came to Alexandria with a large army. He was an Arian, and the people suspected a plot. Athanasius asked him if he brought any message from the Emperor; Syrianus replied that he had none. He was then reminded that Constantius had promised to leave Alexandria in peace. To this he agreed, but gave no reason for his presence. Things went on as usual for three weeks, when the blow that all had been expecting fell.

It was midnight, and the Bishop was holding a vigil service in the Church of St. Theonas, when suddenly shouts and cries broke the silence of the night. Syrianus with five thousand men had surrounded the building, determined to take the Patriarch, alive or dead.

In the dim light of the sanctuary Athanasius sat on the Bishop's throne, calm and unmoved in the midst of the tumult. "Read the 135th Psalm," he said to one of the deacons, "and when it is finished, all will leave the church." The words rang out through the building with their message of hope and confidence and were answered by the people:

"Praise the Lord, for He is good: for His mercy endureth forever.

"Praise ye the God of gods: for His mercy endureth forever."

Those who were nearest the Bishop pressed

him to escape. "The shepherd's place is with his flock," he answered firmly.

Hardly was the Psalm ended when the soldiers rushed in with drawn swords. Many of the people fled; others were trampled underfoot or slain.

Athanasius sat still, his hands folded in prayer. Again they urged him to flee. "Not until all have left the church," he replied.

In desperation, the clergy and monks ended by taking the matter into their own hands. Seizing Athanasius in their arms, they bore him out of the church, passing right through the midst of the soldiers, who were searching everywhere for the Patriarch. It seemed, indeed, as Athanasius himself said later, as if God had covered their eyes.

Into the darkness of the winter's night he fled, an exile and a fugitive once more.

Chapter 8

THE INVISIBLE PATRIARCH

IT was indeed the hour of darkness, and it seemed as if the powers of evil were let loose upon the world. The Arians, with the Emperor on their side, were carrying everything before them. Nearly all the Bishops who had upheld the Nicene faith were in exile or in prison.

St. Antony, over a hundred years old, was on his deathbed. His monks, crowding around the dying Saint, groaned over the evil days that had befallen the Church.

"Fear not," replied the old man, "for this power is of the earth and cannot last. As for the sufferings of the Church, was it not so from the beginning, and will it not be so until the end? Did not the Master Himself say, 'They have persecuted Me, they will persecute you also'? Did not the 'perils from false brethren' begin even in the lifetime of those who had been the companions of Christ? And yet, did not the Master Himself promise that, although she must live in the midst of persecution, He would be with His

Church forever and that the gates of H
not prevail against her?"

With these words of hope and comfort
lips, St. Antony passed to his reward, and they
laid him in his lonely desert grave. His coat of
sheepskin, given him by Athanasius long years
before, he sent with his dying blessing to the
Patriarch, who cherished it as his most precious
possession.

The Alexandrians had not given in without a
struggle. They had protested openly against the
violence of Syrianus, proclaiming throughout the
city that Athanasius was their true Patriarch and
that they would never acknowledge another. It
was of no use; a new reign of terror began in
which all who refused to accept the Arian creed
were treated as criminals. Men and women were
seized and scourged; some were slain. Athanasius was denounced as a "runaway, an evildoer,
a cheat and an impostor, deserving of death."
Letters came from the Emperor ordering all the
churches in the city to be given up to the Arians and requiring the people to receive without
objections the new Patriarch whom he would
shortly send them.

As time went on, things grew worse. The
churches were invaded; altars, vestments and
books were burned and incense thrown on the
flames. An ox was sacrificed in the sanctuary;

priests, monks and nuns were seized and tortured; the houses of the faithful were broken into and robbed. Bishops were driven into exile and their sees filled by Arians, those who were ready to give the most money being generally chosen. Some of them were even pagans; the people were ready to bear any suffering rather than hold communion with them.

When the Emperor Constantius considered that the resistance of the Alexandrians had been sufficiently broken, he addressed them in a conciliatory letter.

Now that the impostor had been driven out, he said, he was about to send them a Patriarch above praise. They would find in the venerable George of Cappadocia the wisest of teachers, one who was fit in every way to lead them to the kingdom of Heaven and to raise their hearts from earthly to heavenly things.

The "venerable" George was not unknown to them—by repute, at least. He had begun his career as seller of pork to the Roman army. It was a position in which a clever man might have made a comfortable fortune. But George was not a clever man, and he was in too great a hurry to get rich. Such impudent dishonesty as his could not pass unnoticed; a precipitate flight alone saved him from a State prison. He was said to have been ordained a priest by the Arians before he was even a Christian. In that case he was no priest, but a useful tool in their hands, for he was capable of anything.

Ignorant and unlettered, he had studied neither theology nor the Scriptures; he was, moreover, a man of bad life, heartless, cruel and greedy. His aim both as Patriarch and as pork-butcher was to make money—as much and as quickly as possible. This was the "wise teacher who was to raise them from the things of earth to those of Heaven." The faithful, with true instinct, prepared for the worst.

They had not long to wait. Even Gregory had been humane compared with George of Cappadocia. Monasteries were burned down; Bishops, priests, virgins, widows—all, in fact, who were faithful to the Church—were insulted, tortured or slain. Many died in consequence of the treatment they had received; others were forced into compliance. The troops of the Emperor, with an Arian at their head, were there to do George's bidding.

The new Patriarch, undisturbed by the sufferings of his victims, was busy enriching himself. Gradually he got control of all the trades in the city; he even made himself chief undertaker and passed a law by which those who dared to bury their dead in a coffin not of his providing could be severely punished. That his coffins cost a small fortune was only to be expected. At the end of two years he had exhausted the patience of the Alexandrians, pagans and Christians alike. There was a popular rising, in which the Patriarch, not having the qualities of a hero, fled for his life. For the next three years he wandered about in the East, lending a hand to every Arian scheme.

In the meantime, where was Athanasius? No one knew—or, at least, so it seemed. He had vanished into the darkness of the night. He was invisible, but his voice could not be silenced, and it was a voice that moved the world. Treatise after treatise in defense of the true Faith; letter after letter—to the Bishops of Egypt, to his friends and to the faithful—was carried far and wide by the hands of trusty messengers. The Arians had the Roman Emperor on their side, but the pen of Athanasius was more powerful than the armies of Constantius.

"God will comfort you," he wrote to his people in Alexandria on hearing that the churches were in the hands of the Arians. "If they have the temples, you have the Faith of the Apostles. If they are in the place, they are far from the Faith; but you, even if you are cast out from the churches, possess the Faith in your hearts. Which is the greater, the place or the Faith? The place is good only when the Faith of the Apostles is taught there; it is holy only when it is the home of holiness."

Rumor said that Athanasius was in hiding in the Thebaid among the monks. The Arians searched the desert foot by foot to find him, but in vain. The monks themselves might have thrown some light upon the matter, but they were silent men, given to prayer and labor; they did not seem to understand what was asked of them, even when questioned with a dagger at their throats.

Silent but faithful, their sentinels were everywhere, watching for the enemy's approach. Athanasius was always warned in time and led by trusty guides to another and a safer place. Sometimes it was only by a hair's breadth that he escaped, but for six years he eluded his enemies. There was not one of the monks who would not gladly have laid down his life for him. He lived among them as one of themselves, and they learned more from him of the religious life than they could teach. As mortified as the holiest among them, always serene and forgetful of self in the midst of hardships and danger, forced sometimes to hide for months in the mountain caves where his only food was what the faithful could bring him, his one thought was the Church. The Arians had made Constantius their spiritual head. They had given him that title of "Eternal" which they had denied to the Son of God. Their Bishops and teachers were everywhere; but Athanasius, like Antony, leaned strongly on Christ's promise.

It would have been madness to return openly to Alexandria while Constantius lived, but several times during those dreadful years Athanasius visited the city in secret and at the risk of his life. In hiding, with a price on his head, he was as formidable an enemy to the Arians as he would have been at Alexandria. His spirit was abroad among the people, encouraging them to persevere, cheering them when downcast, comforting and consoling them in suffering. Though absent, he was their Father and their Bishop still. His voice reached even to distant Gaul, where it encouraged St. Hilary of Poitiers and others, who were striving, even as he was, against heresy.

The Arians were behaving in their usual way —"always slippery, always shuffling," as one who knew them asserted.* At one council, having been accused of denying the Divinity of Christ, they had said: "Let anyone who says that Jesus Christ is a creature like unto other creatures be

---

*The Arians, seeing that their original doctrines were offensive to all Catholic consciences, had now taken up the position known as "Semi-Arian." The Son was *like* the Father, they declared, though not of one substance with Him.

anathema" (accursed). At another which followed it closely—for the Arians and Constantius held a council every few months to gain their ends—they openly stated that Jesus Christ was not God, but a creature. Someone present who had been at the previous council reminded them of the statement they had made on that occasion. "We never meant that Jesus Christ was not a creature," they retorted, "only that he was a different kind of creature from the others!"

In the meantime, as things had quieted down a little in Alexandria, George of Cappadocia resolved to return and see if he could not make a little more money. He was received in an ominous silence, for he was held in abhorrence almost as much by the pagans as by the Christians. A few days later the news reached the city that Constantius was dead and that his nephew Julian had succeeded him as Emperor.

The moment of reckoning had come. George was seized by the pagan population and literally torn to pieces; his body was burned and its ashes scattered to the winds. Thus perished Constantius' "prelate above all praise," and it was not likely that the new Emperor would take much trouble to avenge his death.

Julian, known as "the Apostate," had been a pupil of Eusebius of Nicomedia and a model of youthful piety; but the Christianity of which

Eusebius was a living example had struck but shallow roots. Later he went to Athens, where St. Basil and St. Gregory, the two great doctors of the Church, were his fellow students. "What a viper the Roman Empire is cherishing in its bosom!" exclaimed Gregory, no mean judge of character, "but God grant that I prove a false prophet."

No sooner was Julian crowned Emperor than he threw off the mask and openly declared himself a pagan. The temples of the gods were now rebuilt, sacrifices were offered, and wealth and honors were given to all the Christians who would apostatize.

An edict was published allowing the people to practice whatever religion they chose and recalling everybody who had been banished during the reign of Constantius. This seemed generous, but Julian did not believe in persecution; its results in the past had only been to strengthen the Christians in their faith. His methods were different. Privileges were granted to the pagans which were denied to the Church; the Galileans, as Julian called the Christians, were ridiculed, and paganism was praised as the only religion worthy of educated men.

The results were not what the Emperor had expected, and he complained bitterly that there were so few who responded to his efforts to enlighten them. As for the Church, she knew at least what she had to expect; an open enemy is less dangerous than a false friend.

Chapter 9

A SHORT-LIVED PEACE

ATHANASIUS was quick to take advantage of the decree which allowed the banished Bishops to return to their sees. On the way to Alexandria he stopped to talk over matters with other noble exiles who, like himself, had suffered for the Truth. Many of the faithful had been compelled by force or induced by threats or persuasion to accept the creed of the Arians; what was to be done in order that these weak ones might be brought back to the Faith?

Athanasius and those who with him had been ready to give their lives for the Truth being, like all brave and noble men, gentle and compassionate, they resolved to make it as easy as possible. They announced that absolution would be given freely to all who accepted the Creed of Nicea. Those who had fallen away were mostly good men and true believers who had yielded in a moment of weakness or of fear, or who had been deceived by the protestations of the Arians. They had been thoroughly miserable, but now the proclamation of Athanasius set them free from what had seemed like a bad dream. The Pope himself expressed his approval of Athanasius' forbearance, and the Bishops of the West hastened to follow his example.

In other places, Antioch and Constantinople especially, Arianism had taken deeper root. These were the strongholds of heresy, where the spirit of Eusebius of Nicomedia still prevailed. Men of his stamp were not likely to be ready to enter into communion with that Athanasius whom they had looked upon for years as their mortal enemy, nor was it to be expected that they would allow the true Faith to prevail without a struggle. It was thanks to Athanasius and his untiring efforts that Egypt and Alexandria were still, in the main, true to the Catholic Church.

We can imagine the joy with which the Alexandrians received their exiled Patriarch after his six years' absence. They had been worthy of their Bishop, for they too had made a brave fight for the Faith. Blood had been shed for Christ, and much had been suffered by the Catholics; they could face their Patriarch without shame. Many pagans who had watched the behavior of the Christians under persecution now came forward and asked to join the Church, among them some Greek ladies of noble family whom Athanasius himself instructed and baptized.

News of this reached the ears of the Emperor Julian, who was already furious at the influence that this Christian Bishop of Alexandria was exercising throughout the whole empire. He had hoped that Athanasius' return from exile would have been a cause for division among the people, instead of which it had been the signal for everyone to make peace with his neighbor. Never, he foresaw, as long as the voice of this undaunted champion of the Catholic Church was ringing in the ears of his subjects, would paganism triumph.

There were others who saw the matter in the same light. These were the magicians, diviners, fortune-tellers, all the servants of idolatry who had risen up at Julian's bidding and were swarming in Alexandria as everywhere else. The presence of Athanasius in their midst, they complained to the Emperor, was the ruin of their trade. Even their charms would not work as long as he was near them. There would soon not be a pagan left in the city if he were allowed to remain.

The Patriarch had been barely eight months in Alexandria when the Governor of Egypt received a message from his royal master. "Nothing that I could hear of would give me greater pleasure," he wrote, "than the news that you have driven that miscreant out of the country."

Soon after, the Alexandrians themselves were addressed. "We have allowed the Galileans," wrote Julian, "to return to their country, but not to their churches. Nevertheless, we hear that Athanasius, with his accustomed boldness, has replaced himself on what they call his 'episcopal throne.' We therefore order him to leave the town at once or take the consequences."

The Governor of Egypt, who knew the affection of the Alexandrians for their Patriarch, dared not take any steps against him; the citizens in the meantime had addressed a letter to the Emperor, begging him to reconsider the matter and to leave Athanasius in his see. This only served to anger Julian the more.

"I am painfully surprised that you Alexandrians," he wrote, "who have the great god Serapis and Isis his Queen for your patrons, should ask permission to keep such a man in your midst. I can only hope that those of the citizens who are wiser have not been consulted and that this is the action of a few. I blush to think that any of you could call himself a Galilean. I order Athanasius to leave not only Alexandria, but Egypt."

The Governor also received a curt message.

"If the enemy of the gods, Athanasius, remains in Egypt after the kalends of December," it ran, "you and your troops shall pay a hundred pounds in gold. The gods are despised and I am insulted."

Julian, however, had not much confidence in the Governor, or in the Alexandrians either. In order to make things doubly sure, messengers of his own were sent to Alexandria with orders to put the Patriarch to death.

The people were inconsolable, but Athanasius comforted them. "This time it is only a passing cloud," he said; "it will soon be over." Then, recommending his flock to the most trusted of his clergy, he left the city, an exile once more. It was not a moment too soon. Scarcely had he vanished when the messengers of Julian arrived.

"Where is Athanasius?" they asked; but a grim silence was the only answer.

The Patriarch, in the meantime, had reached the Nile; on the banks of the river a boat was waiting; he entered it, and they rowed swiftly upstream toward the Thebaid.

It was a dangerous moment, but the faithful were watching. A message was brought to the fugitives that soldiers of the Emperor who had orders to seize and kill the Saint had learned his whereabouts and had sworn to overtake him. They implored him to land and take refuge in the desert.

"No," said Athanasius; "turn the boat's head and row toward Alexandria." They thought he was mad, but dared not disobey his orders.

"He who is for us is greater than he who is against us," he said, smiling at their terrified faces. Presently the Imperial boat came in sight, rowing hard in pursuit of the fugitive.

"Have you seen Athanasius? Is he far off?" they shouted, as the little boat drew near.

"He is quite close," answered the Patriarch calmly; "press on."

The crew bent to their oars, the skiff was soon out of sight, but needless to say they did not find their prey. As for Athanasius, he continued his journey to Alexandria, where he landed once more, remaining there for a few days in hiding before he set out for the deserts of the Thebaid.

"The enemy of the gods" had been gotten rid of—for a time, at least, but Julian had still to wait for the triumph of paganism. The gods themselves seemed to be against him. Never had a year been so unlucky as that which followed the banishment of Athanasius. There were earthquakes everywhere; Nicea and Nicomedia were reduced to ruins and Constantinople severely damaged. An extraordinary tidal wave swept over the lower part of the city of Alexandria, leaving shells and seaweed on the roofs of the houses. Famine and plague followed, and it was remarked that the famine seemed to dog the steps of the Emperor wherever he went. People dreaded his arrival in their city; at Antioch, where he stayed for a considerable time, the sufferings were terrible. Julian ordered sacrifices to the gods. So many white oxen were slain that it was said that soon there would be none left in the empire; but still things did not improve.

Julian had begun by being tolerant, but disappointment was making him savage. It was all the fault of the Galileans, he declared. He ordered the Christian soldiers in his army to tear the Cross from Constantine's sacred standard, and he put them to death when they refused. Many Christian churches were closed, and the sacred vessels of the altar seized and profaned. Those who dared resist were imprisoned or slain. Wine that had been offered to the gods was thrown into the public wells and fountains, and all the food that was sold in the markets was defiled in the same way. Two of his officers who complained of this profanation were put to death —not for their religion, Julian hastened to explain, but for their insolence.

The Emperor posed as a philosopher. His long, dirty nails and ragged, uncombed hair and beard were intended to impress his subjects with the wisdom of a man so absorbed in learning that he was above such things as cleanliness. Unfortunately, they had just the opposite effect, and the people made fun of him. They laughed at his sacrifices, where he was often to be seen tearing open with his own hands the bleeding victim to see if he could read inside the signs of success or failure. They laughed at his writings in praise of the gods, where he represented himself as receiving compliments from them all. They laughed at his short stature, at his narrow shoulders and at the huge steps he took in walking, as if, they said, he had been the near relation of one of Homer's giants.

Julian revenged himself upon them in his writings—satires in which Constantine, the first Christian Emperor, was especially held up to ridicule. The Galileans were at the bottom of this as of all other contradictions, he declared, and continued to vent his spleen upon the Christians. It was the last stand of ancient paganism before it died out forever.

Chapter 10

THE LAST EXILE

IT was not safe for Athanasius to remain long in the neighborhood of Alexandria, for the pagans were now having it all their own way. Two of the bravest and most faithful of his clergy had been seized and exiled, and Julian's troops were searching everywhere for the Patriarch. Athanasius made his way to the Thebaid, where he was received with all the old enthusiasm. Under cover of the night, he came up the river to Hermopolis, intending to stay there for some time to preach to the people. The banks of the river were crowded with bishops, monks and clergy who had come out to welcome their Father.

Athanasius landed and, mounted on an ass led by Theodore, Abbot of Tabenna, proceeded to the town escorted by a vast throng of people carrying torches and singing hymns of praise. Here he dismounted, and the monks asked him for his blessing.

"Blessed indeed and worthy of all praise are

these men who carry always the cross of the Lord," he replied.

After having stayed for some time at Hermopolis, he went with the Abbot Theodore to his monastery of Tabenna, where he was already beloved by all. He took the keenest interest in everything that related to the religious life, even to the work of the humblest brother. "It is these men, devoted to humility and obedience," he would often say, "who are our fathers, rather than we theirs."

Round about him lay the great cities of ancient Egypt—"Thebes of the Hundred Gates" and Memphis, the old capital of the kingdom—cities of the dead whose glories had already passed away. The glory that these men had come to seek in their humble monasteries was one which is eternal. The things of this world were small and fleeting to those who lived in the thought of eternity.

It was a country full of holy memories. On the banks of that Nile that flowed so tranquilly among the ancient cities of Egypt, Moses himself had stood lifting hands of prayer for the deliverance of his people. Later, the Salvation of the world Himself had come to dwell for a time beside it, sowing the seeds that were now bringing forth so great a harvest.

It was midsummer, and Athanasius was at

Arsinoe when the news came that the enemy was on his track once more. The Abbot Theodore, who was visiting the Patriarch, persuaded him to embark in his covered boat and to return with him to Tabenna. Tide and wind were against them; the monks had to land and tow the boat; progress was slow, and the soldiers of Julian were not far off. Athanasius was absorbed in prayer, preparing for the martyr's death that, this time at least, seemed very near.

"Fear not," said one of the monks called Ammon, "for God is our protection."

"I have no fear," answered Athanasius; "for many long years I have suffered persecution, and never has it disturbed the peace of my soul. It is a joy to suffer, and the greatest of all joys is to give one's life for Christ."

There was a silence during which all gave themselves to prayer. As the Abbot Theodore besought God to save their Patriarch, it was suddenly made known to him by a divine revelation that at that very moment the Emperor Julian had met his death in battle against the Persians, and that he had been succeeded by Jovian, a Christian and a Catholic. At once he told the good news to Athanasius, advising him to go without delay to the new Emperor and ask to be restored to his see.

In the meantime they had arrived in safety at

Tabenna, where the monks had assembled with joy on hearing of Athanasius' approach. Great was their sorrow when they learned that he had only come to bid them farewell. They gathered around him weeping, begging that he would remember them in his prayers. "If I forget thee, O Jerusalem," cried Athanasius in the words of the Psalmist, "let my right hand be forgotten."

The Emperor Jovian had been an officer in the Roman Army, where his cheerful good nature had so endeared him to the soldiers that he was proclaimed Emperor immediately on Julian's death. There was no need to plead for justice with such a man; scarcely had Athanasius arrived in Alexandria when he received a cordial letter from the Emperor himself.

"Jovian—to Athanasius, the faithful servant of God," it ran. "As we are full of admiration for the holiness of your life and your zeal in the service of Christ our Saviour, we take you from this day forth under our royal protection. We are aware of the courage which makes you count as nothing the heaviest labors, the greatest dangers, the sufferings of persecution and the fear of death. You have fought faithfully for the Truth and edified the whole Christian world, which looks to you as a model of every virtue. It is therefore our desire that you should return to your See and teach the doctrine of salvation.

Come back to your people, feed the flock of Christ and pray for our person, for it is through your prayers that we hope for the blessing of God."

Another letter followed shortly afterward from the Emperor, asking Athanasius to tell him plainly what was the true faith of the Catholic Church and inviting him to visit him at Antioch.

The faith of Nicea was alone to be believed and held, replied the Patriarch; it was that of the whole Catholic world, with the exception of a few men who still held the doctrines of Arius. Nevertheless, he thought it prudent to accept the Emperor's invitation and set out shortly afterward for Antioch. It was well that he did so for the Arians were already on the spot. They had brought with them a man called Lucius in the hope that they would be able to induce Jovian to name him Patriarch of Alexandria in place of Athanasius.

"We are Alexandrians," they declared, "and we beseech your Majesty to give us a Bishop."

"I have already ordered Athanasius to return to his See," was the reply.

"We have proofs against him," they said; "he was condemned and banished by Constantine and Constantius of blessed memory."

"All that was ten or twenty years ago," answered the Emperor; "it is too late to rake it up again now. Besides, I know all about it—by whom he was accused and how he was banished. You need say no more."

The Arians persisted. "Give us whomever you like as Patriarch," they said, "as long as it is not Athanasius. No one in the town will hold communion with him."

"I have heard a very different story," said Jovian; "his teaching is greatly appreciated."

"His teaching is well enough," they retorted, "but his heart is full of malice."

"For his heart he must answer to God, who alone knows what is in it," replied the Emperor; "it is enough for me if his teaching is good."

The Arians at last lost patience. "He calls us heretics!" they exclaimed indignantly.

"That is his duty and the duty of all those who guard the flock of Christ" was the only reply they got.

The Emperor received Athanasius with the deepest respect and listened eagerly to all he had to say on the subject of the true Faith.

After a short stay in Antioch, the Patriarch returned to Alexandria, where he related to the people the success of his enterprise and spoke much in praise of the new Emperor. Their joy was not destined to be lasting. Jovian had been but a few months on the throne when he died suddenly on his way from Antioch to Constan-

tinople. He was succeeded by Valentinian, who
unfortunately for the peace of the Church, chose
his brother Valens to help him in the government, taking the West for his own share of the
Empire and leaving the East to his brother.

Valens, who was both weak and cruel, had an
Arian wife and declared at once in favor of the
Arians. The East was once more to be the scene
of strife and persecution. The Emperor, who had
not yet been baptized, received the Sacrament
at the hands of Eudoxius, the Arian Bishop of
Constantinople, a worthy successor of Eusebius,
who, in the middle of the ceremony, made Valens
take an oath that he would remain faithful to
the Arians and pursue the Catholics with every
rigor.

The Emperor thus won over, the Arians began
to persecute and slander those who were faithful to the Church; several were even put to death.
The Catholics, in desperation, resolved at last
to send an embassy to Valens to ask for justice,
eighty priests and clerics being chosen to make
the petition.

The Emperor, who pretended to listen patiently
to their complaints, had given secret orders to
Modestus, the Prefect of the Pretorian Guard,
to put them all to death. Modestus was as cruel
as his master; but even in Nicomedia, where
Arius and Eusebius had been so active in preach-

ing heresy, the bulk of the people remained true to the Faith of Nicea. Such a wholesale slaughter of innocent ecclesiastics would be almost certain to cause a rising; the thing must be done secretly.

Summoning the doomed men to appear before him, Modestus informed them that the Emperor had sentenced them to banishment. Glad to suffer something for the Faith, they received the news with joy and were promptly embarked on a ship which was supposedly to carry them to the country of their exile. The crew, however, had received their orders from Modestus. They set the ship on fire and escaped in the only boat, leaving the eighty martyrs to perish in the flames. After this, it was evidently useless to appeal to Valens for justice.

The Governors of the different provinces soon received orders to drive out all the Bishops banished by Constantius who had returned during the reign of Julian. The people of Alexandria, however, protested that Athanasius had not returned in the reign of Julian but had been personally recalled by Jovian. The Governor of Egypt dared not insist, for the citizens had gathered in force, determined to defend their Bishop; but he warned the Emperor of the Catholic spirit of the Alexandrians.

A few days later, Athanasius left the city to

stay for a short time in a country house in the neighborhood. It was a providential thing that he did so. That very night the Governor, with a body of armed troops, broke into the church where the Patriarch was usually to be found at prayer. They searched everywhere and were much astonished to find that their prey had escaped them. Athanasius, in the meantime, warned by friends, had concealed himself in his father' tomb, a fairly large vault, where a man migh remain for some time in hiding. The secret wa well kept by the faithful, who brought food to the Patriarch during the night and kept him informed of all that was passing in the city. Fo four long months he remained in concealment at the end of which time the Governor, fearin an outbreak among the people—for the whol of Egypt was in a ferment—persuaded Valens t let him return in peace to his see.

Chapter 11

THE TRUCE OF GOD

ATHANASIUS was back once more in the midst of his people. This time they were determined to keep him at any cost, as they gave the Arians to understand a year later when Lucius, the man who had been recommended to Jovian as a suitable Patriarch, ventured to make his appearance in Alexandria. No sooner did the people hear of his arrival than they surrounded the house where he was lodging, and it would have gone ill with him had not the Governor, with an armed troop, rescued him and hurried him out of Egypt. The roar against him that rose from the multitude as he was escorted by a strong guard out of the city completely cured him of any desire to return, and Athanasius was left in peace for the remaining years of his life.

He had grown old, and his strength was failing, but his soul, still young and vigorous, was undaunted and heroic as ever. The seven last years of his rule at Alexandria were no more years of rest than those which had gone before.

He was one of the few bishops still living who had been present at the Council of Nicea. The whole Catholic world, West as well as East, venerated him as a Confessor of the Faith and looked to him for advice and help.

His pen was still busy. One of his first acts on his return to Alexandria was to write the life of St. Antony of the Desert, a last tribute of love and gratitude to the memory of his dear old friend. The book was eagerly read; we are told in the *Confessions of St. Augustine* how two young officers of the Imperial army, finding it on the table of a certain hermitage near Milan and reading it, were so inspired by enthusiasm for the religious life that they embraced it then and there.

In the other parts of the Eastern empire Valens and the Arians were still at work, and persecution was raging as of old. Many of the persecuted Bishops looked to Athanasius for the comfort and encouragement which they never sought in vain. He was always ready to forget the past and to make advances even to those who had been his bitterest enemies. Let them only accept the Creed of Nicea, he said, and he would admit them to communion.

There was a splendid chivalry about the man who could so generously hold out the right hand of fellowship to those who had never ceased to plot his ruin. The triumph of truth and the salvation of souls was his first, and indeed his only thought; everything else could be safely forgotten. Unfortunately, it was not so with the leaders of the Arians, and they refused to respond to his appeal. There were, however, among them good men who had been deceived into signing false creeds and who were beginning to see things in their true light. Many of these were received back into the Church and became true and firm friends of the Patriarch, who was always more ready to see the good in his fellowmen than the evil.

God had not given to everyone the clear instinct and the wide learning of an Athanasius. It was sometimes really difficult to see where the truth lay, for the Arians always tried to conceal their real doctrines from those who would have shrunk from them in horror. Their old trick of declaring that they believed all that the Church believed had led many astray. For misled men such as these, honest and true of heart, Athanasius had the greatest compassion and sympathy; they could always count on his help.

He carried the same large-mindedness into the affairs of his government. A certain Bishop of Libya having grown too old to carry out his duties to the people's satisfaction, they asked that he should be replaced by a younger and more capable prelate. But they had not the patience to wait till the affair was settled. Siderius, a young Christian officer stationed in the province, had won the hearts of all by his virtue and wisdom; he, and none other, they resolved, should take the place of the old man. A Bishop called Philo was accordingly persuaded to consecrate Siderius, a thing he had no right to do, as the Patriarch had not been consulted; neither were there two other Bishops present, as was required for a lawful consecration.

The news of this irregular proceeding came in due time to the ears of Athanasius, who sent someone to inquire into the matter. Finding, however, that Siderius was worthy in every way of the position in which he had been placed, he ratified the choice of the people and showed much favor to the young Bishop.

Yet a few years later he was ready to brave the Emperor's anger by excommunicating the Governor of Libya, a man whose cruelty and evil deeds had made him hateful to all. As the man was a native of Cappadocia, Athanasius wrote to St. Basil, the Archbishop of Caesarea in Cappadocia, to tell him what he had done. St. Basil replied that he had published the excommunication throughout his diocese and forbidden anyone to hold communion with the unhappy man. He asked Athanasius to pray for him and his people, for the Arians were hard at work among them.

Valens, in the meantime, had decided that the whole empire must be Arian and was trying to obtain his end by force. Arian prelates arrived in Caesarea, and Modestus, Prefect of the Pretorian Guard, informed the Archbishop that he must admit them to communion under pain of banishment. St. Basil, having resisted the order, was brought up before the Prefect's tribunal.

"Why will you not accept the Emperor's religion?" asked the latter. "Do you think it is a small thing to be of our communion?"

"Although you are Prefects and powerful people," answered the Archbishop, "you are not to be more respected than God."

"Do you not know that I have power to drive you into exile, even to take your life?" cried Modestus in a rage.

"I am God's pilgrim," was the answer; "all countries are the same to me, and death is a good gift when it brings me to Him for whom I live and work."

"No one has ever spoken so boldly to me before," replied Modestus, astonished.

"You have probably never met a Christian Bishop before," said Basil, "or he would certainly have answered you as I have done. In all other things we are meek and obedient, but when it is a question of God's worship, we look to Him alone. Threats are of no use, for suffering in His service is our greatest delight."

"Would you not like to have the Emperor in your congregation?" asked Modestus. "It would be so easy. You have only to strike that word 'Consubstantial' out of your creed."

"Gladly would I see the Emperor in my church," said Basil; "it is a great thing to save a soul; but as for changing my creed, I would not alter a letter for the whole world."

The persecution continued, and Basil addressed himself once more to Athanasius, asking for prayers and guidance. "We are persuaded," he wrote, "that your leadership is our sole remaining comfort in our distress. By the power of your prayers, by the wisdom of your counsels, you are able to carry us through this fearful storm, as all are sure who have in any way made trial of your goodness. Wherefore cease not to pray for our souls and to stir us up by letters; if you only knew how these benefit us, you would never let pass an opportunity of writing. If it were given to me, through your prayers, once to see you, to profit by your gifts and to add to the history of my life a meeting with such a great and apostolic soul, surely I should consider that the loving mercy of God has given me a compensation for all the ills with which my life has been afflicted."

In 366 Pope Liberius died and was succeeded by Pope St. Damasus, a man of strong character and holy life. Two years later, in a council of the Church, it was decreed that no Bishop should be consecrated unless he held the Creed of Nicea. Athanasius was overwhelmed with joy on hearing this decision. The triumph of the cause for which he had fought so valiantly was now assured.

Athanasius' life was drawing to an end. Five years later, after having governed his diocese for forty-eight years—years of labor, endurance and suffering—he passed peacefully into the presence of that Lord for whose sake he had counted all his tribulations as joy.

From his earliest youth Athanasius had stood forth as the champion of Truth and defender of the Faith—a gallant warrior who had not laid down his arms until the day of his death. Where a weaker man would have lost courage, he had stood firm; suffering had only served to temper his spirit, as steel is tempered by the fire. Among men who were capable of every compromise he had remained loyal and true, and few have been more loved or hated than he. To his own people he was not only their Bishop, but a Saint, an ascetic, a martyr in all but deed; above all, he was an intensely lovable personality, whose very greatness of soul only made him more compassionate. To the outside world he was a guiding light, a beacon pointing straight to God and Heaven. He was a living example of the truth that a man may be large-minded and yet strong; that he may hate error, yet love the erring—stand like a rock against heresy, yet be full of compassion for heretics.

Scarcely was Athanasius dead when he was honored as a Saint. Six years after his death, St. Gregory Nazianzen speaks of him in one breath with the patriarchs, prophets and martyrs who had fought for the Faith and won the crown of glory. His influence is with us to this day, his memory lingers in the words of that Nicene Creed which was his war cry; for it is largely owing to his valor that we possess it still. And through all his works breathes the same spirit—the spirit that nerved him to fight and suffer—an intense love and devotion to Him who was the Lord and Master of his life—Jesus Christ, the same yesterday, today and forever.

If you have enjoyed this book, consider making your next selection from among the following . . .

Prices subject to change.

The Secret of Mary. *St. Louis De Montfort* 5.00
St. Maria Goretti. *Fr. Poage, C. P.* 6.00
Stories of Padre Pio. *Tangari* 8.00
Miraculous Images of Our Lady. *Joan Carroll Cruz* 20.00
Miraculous Images of Our Lord. *Cruz* 13.50
Brief Catechism for Adults. *Fr. Cogan* 9.00
Raised from the Dead. *Fr. Hebert* 16.50
Autobiography of St. Margaret Mary 5.00
Thoughts and Sayings of St. Margaret Mary 5.00
The Voice of the Saints. *Comp. by Francis Johnston* 7.00
The 12 Steps to Holiness and Salvation. *St. Alphonsus* . . . 7.50
The Rosary and the Crisis of Faith. *Cirrincione/Nelson* . . . 2.00
Sin and Its Consequences. *Cardinal Manning* 6.00
Fourfold Sovereignty of God. *Cardinal Manning* 5.00
Dialogue of St. Catherine of Siena. *Transl. Thorold* 10.00
Catholic Answer to Jehovah's Witnesses. *D'Angelo* 12.00
Twelve Promises of the Sacred Heart. (100 cards) 5.00
Life of St. Aloysius Gonzaga. *Fr. Meschler* 12.00
The Love of Mary. *D. Roberto* 8.00
Begone Satan. *Fr. Vogl* 3.00
The Prophets and Our Times. *Fr. R. G. Culleton* 13.50
St. Therese, The Little Flower. *John Beevers* 6.00
Mary, The Second Eve. *Cardinal Newman* 3.00
Devotion to Infant Jesus of Prague. *Booklet* 75
The Wonder of Guadalupe. *Francis Johnston* 7.50
Apologetics. *Msgr. Paul Glenn* 10.00
Baltimore Catechism No. 1 . . . . 3.50
Baltimore Catechism No. 2 . . . . 4.50
Baltimore Catechism No. 3 . . . . 8.00
An Explanation of the Baltimore Catechism. *Kinkead* 16.50
Bible History. *Schuster* 13.50
Blessed Eucharist. *Fr. Mueller* 9.00
Catholic Catechism. *Fr. Faerber* 7.00
The Devil. *Fr. Delaporte* 6.00
Evidence of Satan in the Modern World. *Cristiani* 10.00
Fifteen Promises of Mary. (100 cards) 5.00
Life of Anne Catherine Emmerich. 2 vols. *Schmoeger* . . . 37.50
Life of the Blessed Virgin Mary. *Emmerich* 16.50
Prayer to St. Michael. (100 leaflets) 5.00
Prayerbook of Favorite Litanies. *Fr. Hebert* 10.00
Purgatory Explained. *Schouppe* 13.50
Purgatory Explained. (pocket, unabr.). *Schouppe* 9.00
Trustful Surrender to Divine Providence. *Bl. Claude* 5.00
Prices subject to change.

Prices subject to change.

Story of a Soul. *St. Therese of Lisieux* 8.00
Catholic Children's Treasure Box Books 1-10 . . . . 35.00
Prayers and Heavenly Promises. *Cruz*. 5.00
Magnificent Prayers. *St. Bridget of Sweden* 2.00
The Happiness of Heaven. *Fr. J. Boudreau* 8.00
The Glories of Mary. *St. Alphonsus Liguori* 16.50
The Glories of Mary. (pocket, unabr.). *St. Alphonsus* 10.00
The Curé D'Ars. *Abbé Francis Trochu* 21.50
Humility of Heart. *Fr. Cajetan da Bergamo* 8.50
Love, Peace and Joy. (St. Gertrude). *Prévot* 7.00
Père Lamy. *Biver* 12.00
Passion of Jesus & Its Hidden Meaning. *Groenings* 15.00
Mother of God & Her Glorious Feasts. *Fr. O'Laverty* 10.00
Song of Songs—A Mystical Exposition. *Fr. Arintero* 20.00
Love and Service of God, Infinite Love. *de la Touche* . . . 12.50
Life & Work of Mother Louise Marg. *Fr. O'Connell* 12.50
Martyrs of the Coliseum. *O'Reilly* 18.50
Rhine Flows into the Tiber. *Fr. Wiltgen* 15.00
What Catholics Believe. *Fr. Lawrence Lovasik* 5.00
Who Is Therese Neumann? *Fr. Charles Carty* 2.00
Summa of the Christian Life. 3 Vols. *Granada* 36.00
St. Francis of Paola. *Simi and Segreti.* 8.00
The Rosary in Action. *John Johnson* 9.00
Is It a Saint's Name? *Fr. William Dunne* 2.50
St. Martin de Porres. *Giuliana Cavallini* 12.50
Douay-Rheims New Testament. *Paperbound* 15.00
St. Catherine of Siena. *Alice Curtayne* 13.50
Blessed Virgin Mary. *Liguori* 4.50
Chats With Converts. *Fr. M. D. Forrest* 10.00
The Stigmata and Modern Science. *Fr. Charles Carty* 1.50
St. Gertrude the Great 1.50
Thirty Favorite Novenas 75
Brief Life of Christ. *Fr. Rumble* 2.00
Catechism of Mental Prayer. *Msgr. Simler* 2.00
On Freemasonry. *Pope Leo XIII* 1.50
Thoughts of the Curé D'Ars. *St. John Vianney* 2.00
Incredible Creed of Jehovah Witnesses. *Fr. Rumble* 1.50
St. Pius V—His Life, Times, Miracles. *Anderson.* 5.00
St. Dominic's Family. *Sr. Mary Jean Dorcy* 24.00
St. Rose of Lima. *Sr. Alphonsus* 15.00
Latin Grammar. *Scanlon & Scanlon* 16.50
Second Latin. *Scanlon & Scanlon* 12.00
St. Joseph of Copertino. *Pastrovicchi* 6.00
Prices subject to change.

Religious Customs in/Family. *Fr. Weiser, S. J.* 8.00
Mama! Why Did You Kill Us?. *Mondrone* 2.00
St. Maximilian Kolbe—Knight of/Immaculata. *Smith* 6.00
Saint Michael and the Angels. *Approved Sources.* 7.00
Dolorous Passion of Our Lord. *Anne C. Emmerich* 16.50
Our Lady of Fatima's Peace Plan from Heaven. *Booklet* . . .75
Three Ways of the Spiritual Life. *Garrigou-Lagrange* 6.00
Mystical Evolution. 2 Vols. *Fr. Arintero, O.P.* 36.00
St. Catherine Labouré of the Mirac. Medal. *Fr. Dirvin* . . . 13.50
Manual of Practical Devotion to St. Joseph. *Patrignani* . . . 15.00
The Active Catholic. *Fr. Palau* 7.00
Ven. Jacinta Marto of Fatima. *Cirrincione* 2.00
Reign of Christ the King. *Davies* 1.25
St. Teresa of Avila. *William Thomas Walsh* 21.50
Isabella of Spain—The Last Crusader. *Wm. T. Walsh* 20.00
Characters of the Inquisition. *Wm. T. Walsh* 15.00
Philip II. *William Thomas Walsh.* H.B. 37.50
Blood-Drenched Altars—Cath. Comment. Hist. Mexico . . . 20.00
Self-Abandonment to Divine Providence. *de Caussade* . . . 18.00
Way of the Cross. *Liguorian* 1.00
Way of the Cross. *Franciscan* 1.00
Modern Saints—Their Lives & Faces, Bk. 1. *Ann Ball* . . . 18.00
Modern Saints—Their Lives & Faces, Bk. 2. *Ann Ball* . . . 20.00
Divine Favors Granted to St. Joseph. *Pere Binet* 5.00
St. Joseph Cafasso—Priest of the Gallows. *St. J. Bosco* . . 5.00
Catechism of the Council of Trent. *McHugh/Callan* 24.00
Why Squander Illness? *Frs. Rumble & Carty* 2.50
Fatima—The Great Sign. *Francis Johnston* 8.00
Heliotropium—Conformity of Human Will to Divine 13.00
Charity for the Suffering Souls. *Fr. John Nageleisen* 16.50
Devotion to the Sacred Heart of Jesus. *Verheylezoon* 15.00
Fundamentals of Catholic Dogma. *Ott* 21.00
Litany of the Blessed Virgin Mary. (100 cards) 5.00
Who Is Padre Pio? *Radio Replies Press* 2.00
The Life of Christ. 4 Vols. H.B. *Anne C. Emmerich.* 60.00
St. Anthony—The Wonder Worker of Padua. *Stoddard* . . . 5.00
The Precious Blood. *Fr. Faber* 13.50
The Holy Shroud & Four Visions. *Fr. O'Connell* 2.00
Clean Love in Courtship. *Fr. Lawrence Lovasik* 2.50
The Secret of the Rosary. *St. Louis De Montfort* 3.00

At your Bookdealer or direct from the Publisher.
Call Toll Free 1-800-437-5876

Prices subject to change.

ABOUT THE AUTHOR

This book was authored by Mother Frances Alice Monica Forbes, a sister of the Society of the Sacred Heart, Scotland.

The future author was born on March 16, 1869 and was named Alice Forbes. Alice's mother died when she was a child, and her father became the dominant influence in her life, helping to form Alice's virile personality and great capacity for work. She was raised as a Presbyterian.

In 1900 Alice became a Catholic. The Real Presence in the Eucharist had been the big stumbling-block to her conversion, but one day she was hit by the literal truth of Our Lord's words: "This is My Body." Only a few months after her conversion, she entered the Society of the Sacred Heart, becoming a 31-year-old postulant. She seems to have received her vocation at her First Communion, when Our Lord kindled in her heart "the flame of an only love."

In the convent, Sister Forbes used her keen intelligence and strong will to make generously and completely the sacrifices that Our Lord asked of her each day. She put great store by the virtue of obedience. Much of the latter part of her life was spent in illness and suffering, yet she was always kind and uncomplaining—a charming person and a "gallant" soul. Throughout her sufferings the most important thing to her was the love of God. She died in 1936.

Mother Frances Alice Monica Forbes wrote many

books, including a series of interesting short lives of selected Saints called "Standard Bearers of the Faith." One of these books, that on Pope St. Pius X, was very highly regarded by Cardinal Merry del Val, who was a close friend of Pope Pius X.

Other works by Mother Frances Alice Monica Forbes include *St. Ignatius Loyola, St. John Bosco: Friend of Youth, St. Teresa, St. Columba, St. Monica, St. Athanasius, St. Catherine of Siena, St. Benedict, St. Hugh of Lincoln, The Gripfast Series of English Readers* and *The Gripfast Series of History Readers*, various plays, and a number of other books.

The above information is from the book *Mother F. A. Forbes: Religious of the Sacred Heart—Letters and Short Memoir*, by G. L. Sheil (London: The Catholic Book Club, 1948, by arrangement with Longmans, Green & Co., Ltd.).